Helping Children
to be Strong

Also available in the From Birth to Three series:

Helping Children to be Competent Learners
Ann Roberts and Avril Harpley (ed. Sandy Green)
978-1-84312-450-4
1-84312-451-3

Helping Children to be Skilful Communicators
Ann Roberts and Avril Harpley (ed. Sandy Green)
978-1-84312-449-8
1-84312-449-1

Helping Children to Stay Healthy
Ann Roberts and Avril Harpley (ed. Sandy Green)
978-1-84312-448-1
1-84312-448-3

Helping Children to be Strong

From Birth to Three

Ann Roberts and Avril Harpley

Routledge
Taylor & Francis Group

LONDON AND NEW YORK

First published 2007 by Routledge
2 Park Square, Milton Park, Abingdon, Oxon, OX14 4RN

Simultaneously published in the USA and Canada
by Routledge

270 Madison Ave, New York, NY 10016

Routledge is an imprint of the Taylor & Francis Group, an informa business

Typeset in Trade Gothic by FiSH Books, Enfield, Middx.
Printed and bound in Great Britain by TJ International Ltd, Padstow

British Library Cataloguing in Publication Data
A catalogue record for this book is available from the British Library.

Library of Congress Cataloging in Publication Data
A catalogue record for this book has been requested.

ISBN 10: 1-84312-451-3
ISBN 13: 978-1-84312-451-1

Contents

Acknowledgements

We would like to thank the following children and parents who provided some wonderful photographs to be used in this book:

Maria Williams; Antrim, Northern Ireland
Mark Williams; Childminder, Lewisham, London
Laura Henry; Early Years consultant, Childcare consultancy
Anna and Eve, and their parents Gregory and Cath
Poppy and her parents Mick and Leanne, and Grandma Sandra
Lucas and Jago and their parents Debbie and Chris
Nina Khan; Childminder, Thorton Heath, Surrey
The parents of Katie and her brother Mathew
Molly and her granddad, her parents Steven and Donnah. Sisters Kaisha and Fraiyah.

Warm thanks also to the many friends and colleagues who have helped to test run the practical activities.

Ann and Avril

Introduction

Helping young children to develop their personal, social and emotional skills is one of the most important things any practitioner can do. Giving babies and toddlers a disposition to learn is built on self-assurance, high self-esteem and confidence. The process of identifying the core elements of personal, social and emotional development (PSED) is rarely stripped down or consistently investigated. 'We do it all the time' practitioners often say; however, putting it as a specific focus and evaluating, planning and addressing it in a systematic and sustainable way is something quite different. Knowledge and understanding of how babies and young children think and feel is complex and as more research evolves we are often left with even more questions.

This book uses the framework of *Birth to Three Matters* (DfES, 2002) and adds to it some effective everyday suggestions of activities which parents and carers can try with their baby or toddler. Every child is unique and some children develop their speech at different rates. Adults need to act as interested enablers and through acknowledging and encouraging children they will engender confidence. These are the intentions behind the activities and suggestions for children.

In this book the activities are based around easily accessible everyday items in order to encourage practitioners to use these objects to support and reflect the home environment within the setting. Simple role-play opportunities, such as using boxes and cloths, encourage open-ended play and exploration, enabling children to communicate what is in their mind. Imagination, creativity and language are all interconnected.

By posing challenges and questions to staff, readers are invited to reflect on their own practice and think about how they can communicate more effectively with babies and toddlers and assist their developing skills.

Why should we help children to be strong?

Working through phrases chosen from the *Birth to Three Matters* guidelines (currently being incorporated into the new Early Years Foundation Stage, 0–5, due to be launched in 2008) forms the backdrop for this book. This book approaches the areas of personal, social and emotional development by summarising the issues arising from the *Birth to Three Matters* quotes and then provides the practitioner/reader with some ideas of how to translate them into activities.

The practitioner's skill and sensitivity is crucial in this area of learning and being a positive role model to the children is essential. Babies and toddlers must feel safe and trust in those who care for them. Good observational skills, empathy and having dedicated time for professional reflection are needed to consider and meet the needs of each child.

Each child is an individual from the day he is born and has a unique personality with likes and dislikes. Personal, social and emotional development cannot be done in a random manner and no one strategy works for all. Practitioners have to seek and find out what is right for every child in their care. Each time a new baby or toddler joins a setting this process of exploration begins. This book asks each practitioner to re-evaluate her practice and her approach to what is the most important area of development at a most important time in the lives of babies and toddlers.

It may mean looking at the routines, procedures and the qualities that each member of staff brings to the setting.

Sure Start has developed a training package (*Personal, Social and Emotional Development: Birth to Five*, 2006) to raise the standards of training in this area and has passed this on to each Local Authority to develop and use with their practitioners. Staff training requires both thought and action. The section on staff training in this book is intended to provoke discussion and present some suggestions. It is hoped that the team will want to address areas that need to be developed. These areas must have clear intended outcomes that link directly to benefiting babies and toddlers so that they can become strong children.

How to use this book

This book has been written with a practical focus in mind. Practitioners need ideas to use with babies and toddlers. They are busy people and have limited resources at their disposal. The connections made with *Birth to Three Matters* at the beginning of each chapter are designed to support them as they plan and use the documents on a daily basis.

After an introduction, each chapter contains six numbered parts, each one subdivided into sections. The first two sections of each part look at babies and toddlers. The baby section covers from 0 to 18 months and the toddlers' section runs from 18 to 36 months. Both provide practical activities. Obviously, the practitioner will recognise that every child is unique and so adaptations to some of the suggested activities will be necessary. Safety is very important and so cautionary advice is offered throughout the book. If children have specialist needs, readers will need to take these into consideration before using the activities and make an informed safety decision on how to use them in their situation.

Following the activities is a section on the outcomes for the child. The points are designed to help us fully recognise the importance of the child in everything that is offered. If we are intending to help children to become strong learners, we need to assess how well we are doing this from the child's point of view. Ofsted also focuses on this within its inspection framework and so this will assist practitioners in their evaluations and their preparation for an Ofsted visit.

The focus points that follow are to make us as adults draw some thoughts and feelings together about the practical activities, their purpose, the impact they have and how this can all be built on for the child. They are intended to encourage the reader to consider, question and reflect.

Staff discussion is important. Talking about what we do and trying to make sense of it with others helps us to improve the quality and standard of our work. If we want children to become strong, we need to see how our role is fitting into the overall picture and how effective we are being.

Finally, each chapter concludes with a list of references. These references are linked to three key documents: *National Standards for Under 8s Day Care and Childminding (Full Day Care)* (DfES/DWP, 2003); *Birth to Three Matters* (DfES, 2002) and *Every Child Matters* (DfES, 2003). These are intended to assist the reader in making connections between practice and theory. Chapters 1–3 also provide a list of resources which include related books and websites that practitioners might find useful.

References

DfES (Department for Education and Skills) (2002) *Birth to Three Matters: A Framework to Support Children in their Earliest Years.* London: DfES.

DfES (Department for Education and Skills) (2003) *Every Child Matters.* London: DfES.

DfES (Department for Education and Skills)/DWP (Department for Work and Pensions) (2003) *National Standards for Under 8s Day Care and Childminding (Full Day Care).* London: DfES.

Me, myself and I

Introduction

The first chapter of this book, 'Me, myself and I', is about a period of self-discovery and focuses on the development of a child's identity. By the time a child is ready to move on from pre-school he should have developed a secure sense of his own individuality, be aware of his strengths and understand that it is OK to be different.

The role of the practitioner centres on helping the child to develop positive relationships and a feeling of self-worth rather than expecting him to follow a curriculum. Without the security of good self-esteem, confidence and self-worth, formal learning may be delayed. These personal qualities are shaped by the reactions and responses of others as well as the child's own expectations. Initially a child's view of himself in the world is formed by the family who create beliefs, values and attitudes. Once babies and young children enter an early years setting/childcare they encounter a whole new range of behaviours, customs and reactions. This can be upsetting and confusing, although some children learn to live in two cultures at the same time. The situation is eased if practitioners support the children and help them to adjust by making the environment more like home. In order for this to happen practitioners need to work closely with parents/carers in order to understand the families' background and culture. If a family has English as a second language, it is important to discover, and use, essential phrases such as greetings, and words used for physical needs: hunger, sleep and personal hygiene. In this way, they can get to know the children in their care, their interests and family expectations and support them more effectively.

Throughout this book there are sections for staff discussion. This is an important area where the adults can get to know how they each feel and think about the care and education of young children. Areas for reflection are the practitioner's own concept of self-worth, their attitudes, values and prejudices and how this may affect their relationships with the children in their care.

1. Identity

> Young babies become aware of themselves as separate from
> others, learning also that they have influence *upon* and are
> influenced others.
>
> (*Birth to Three Matters*)

Babies

From birth, babies are interested in what is going on around them. During these
early stages of development, the beginning of a sense of self and an awareness of
their identity is closely linked to the responses of their parents and main carers.
As they mature babies begin to realise that they are separate beings and
individuals. This can be observed when babies use their sense of touch and taste;
they suck and chew as they play with their hands and feet. Over time, they gain
greater control of their body and mind and begin to understand these hands and
feet are theirs and they can move them. Babies use their ability to cry to influence
others and communicate their needs to parents and carers.

Practical activities

- Place a treasure basket between two babies and observe carefully. Look for clues that indicate each child's interest. Follow this up by creating a treasure basket for each child based on these observations. Use a luggage label containing the babies' photograph to identify the baskets.

- Focus on providing sensory activities that encourage babies to be aware of their hands and feet. For example, provide individual trays of sand and bowls for water play, place ice-cubes or aromas in the water, use soft feathers that tickle. Note how the babies explore these natural resources and how they respond to them.

- Create an area containing mirrors and position the babies so that they can see their own reflections. This is one way that demonstrates they have self-awareness and know 'It's me!'

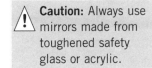 **Caution:** Always use mirrors made from toughened safety glass or acrylic.

- Observe babies' expressions and actions when they attempt to influence others. Capture these significant moments on film.

Toddlers

As babies mature and become toddlers their sense of self becomes stronger. It is essential that this is a positive experience. Feeling comfortable, or good, about oneself is the foundation for high self-esteem and influences a child's position in society, his attitudes and his disposition for learning.

It is the core of personal, social and emotional development.

Practical activities

- Identity is very important. Make name labels personal and specific to each child by including a photograph of the child along with a picture of an item of special significance, such as his teddy or his pet. Ask the child what he would like to include. Learn to pronounce and spell his name correctly.

- Look for ways to show that you respect and value each child's preferences, likes/dislikes and interests. For example, create a specific area where he can display his favourite things, listen carefully when he wants to share his news, be aware of what he likes to eat and who he likes to sit alongside.

- Create a photo wall and have a safety mirror in the centre where the children can see their own reflections.

- Place hats and scarves, clown noses or face paints beside a safety mirror so that the children can interact and try out different 'faces'. Take photos of their 'new look'.

- Develop a time during the day when you come together in small groups to talk about their news, favourite things they have done during the day or would like to do. Help the children to develop their memory skills by recalling activities and events.

- Set up a video loop of the children's activities during the day and show this when parents/carers come to collect their children. Spend time talking with parents/carers pointing out the positive things their children have achieved. Alternatively create a picture/photo board of achievements with appropriate comments such as 'I tied my laces today' or 'I played in the water with my friend'.

Outcomes for the child

- Children understand that they have the power to make an impact on another.
- Beginning to appreciate that they are unique.
- Developing confidence.
- Developing social qualities and forming friendships.

Focus points

If adults label a child's behaviour or character, it can affect his sense of self and the role he plays. For example, if adults refer to a child as 'naughty' or 'silly', he may try to live up to, or down to, that expectation. At around two years of age toddlers begin to establish themselves as separate and this is evident in their language when they start to use pronouns correctly, for example me, mine, you, yours. They also recognise their own gender and often actively seek out same-sex play mates.

Staff discussion

- Encourage key persons to write a short description of each baby/child and try to ensure they capture the individuality of each one. If the name of the child is removed, could another person recognise who it is? Test this out.

- Record significant moments on photographs, such as when the baby realises that her hands and feet are part of her body. Date the photo and share this important stepping stone in development with parents/carers.

- What strategies are used to get to know the children in your care? Are they effective?

● Reflect if any staff bring prejudices or assumptions to the setting, for example they prefer to work with boys rather than girls or only with the 'bright' children or don't like attention seekers. How do you address this to ensure all children are treated equally?

2. Self-awareness

Babies develop an understanding and awareness of themselves, which is influenced by their family, culture, other people and the environment.

(Birth to Three Matters)

Babies

Babies find mirrors fascinating and there are many products available now that can be safely used. Very young babies begin to develop their understanding and awareness of 'self' and the use of safety mirrors can support this. Encourage parents/carers to use these ideas at home. Ensure that there are mirrors situated both indoors and outdoors. Place mirrors on fencing or bushes at the appropriate height. If babies are in their buggies, check the height that the mirror will have to be so that they can see their own reflections easily. If they are outside on mats or blankets or in soft play rings, provide several hand-held mirrors. Safety and appropriate resources are crucial and this is the responsibility of the practitioner.

Practical activities

- Have a safety mirror placed in the baby's cot. These are usually mirrors encased in a prism-shaped sponge that can be attached to the cot itself. This allows the baby to explore the mirror while lying on her tummy.

- Hang reflective items over the nappy-changing area or fix single acrylic mirror tiles or even a budgie mirror with bells on.

- Fix several plastic mirror tiles onto a section of a wall so that babies can look at themselves. Fixing a pull up bar can be very effective.

- Make a 'reflective theme' treasure basket. Include in it shiny spoons, balti dishes, stainless steel items so that babies can see their reflection. Place this basket on a silver car sunscreen protector – to complete the presentation.

Toddlers

An awareness of self is partly formed through the information we receive from the world around us, our social experiences and how others see us and react to us. If this feedback is usually positive, the reaction will be 'I am OK'; however, if there are too many negatives, then a child might think 'I am no good at anything' and this will inhibit confidence and potential. Early childhood is a crucial stage for the development of self-awareness and self-esteem.

Practical activities

- Create an attractive 'welcome' area. Try to arrange to have time to greet each parent/carer and his child with smiles and a few words that make the child feel you are glad he has arrived. If possible, arrange for a staggered entry time to avoid a rush.

- Make time during the beginning of the day for a circle meeting, which encourages the children to have the sense of belonging to the group. Talk about the activities in the room, any news the children wish to share or their special interests. End the day with a circle and discuss what the children have enjoyed, what they feel they have done well, what they would like to do tomorrow. Include your own comments such as 'I really enjoyed being outside today and seeing you all . . .' Don't forget to include some reflections such as 'I did not get all my jobs done today, I was not very well organised; I will make sure I do tomorrow'. This can show the children that it is all right to make a mistake.

- Make a smiley badge to give to those children who have been kind, thoughtful, happy or polite.

- Spray some branches silver and fix them securely into a jam jar. Use circle shapes for each child to make a happy face. When they feel good they hang their face onto the branches; when sad, they can take it off. This can help to promote a dialogue about their feelings. The branches can be used in a similar way to show blossoming friendships or 'special' helpers.

- Turn an area of the room into a gallery to display the children's favourite pieces. Let them decide what should be there. Include their name and a short caption giving details of their achievement such as 'Mark used paint for the first time today'.

Outcomes for the child

- Recognising 'yourself' and understanding 'myself'.
- Playing and experiencing interactions with resources which stimulate a sense of self.
- Developing a sense of belonging.
- Developing respect for own family and culture.
- Understanding that making a mistake is not in itself bad but part of learning.

Focus points

Children engage in role play based on their family situations, what they know and understand about the world. As their social life expands and they widen their experiences, they explore how others behave. It is in this context that they begin to develop an awareness of how and where they fit in. When they are able to develop a realistic view of themselves and can accept their good qualities, their self-esteem is strengthened. Good self-esteem is strongly linked to happiness, and success boosts self-esteem.

Staff discussion

- Evaluate resources to see if they support the cultural/ethnic mix of the children in the setting. Discuss what other items could be used to help support the children's self-awareness and identity.
- Imagine how the baby room looks from the babies' point of view. What can they see or access? How relevant is it to their lives?
- Examine ways that adults can enable learning and empower children to become more independent and autonomous.

- Attend craft shows and art exhibitions and browse specialist shops (DIY and large supermarkets) to see new products that are on the market. Be inventive and look for items that will stimulate the children.

- Do staff develop their knowledge and understanding of other cultures? Are they fully aware of what is offensive to some cultures so that they do not offend a family through ignorance? How do they build up a respectful relationship with parents and carers?

- Encourage staff to be aware of the religious environment that is part of the children's lives. Try to organise visits to their places of worship: temples, mosques, churches, etc. Ensure when visiting that staff are aware of what to wear and how to behave in order not to offend.

- Hold events to support cultural high points in family lives. Working with the families to do this together can be effective and meaningful.

- Ask yourself how many times a day you use negative/positive comments when talking to children?

3. Similarities and differences

Young children learn they have similarities and differences that connect them to, and distinguish them from, others.

(*Birth to Three Matters*)

Babies

The way an effective practitioner interacts with a baby can have a tremendously positive effect on her self-image and is instrumental in helping her develop into a strong child. Even though practitioners aim to treat all children equally, they may have personal preferences and are drawn to babies with certain characteristics and personalities and not others. Some babies are very responsive and are easier to get to know than others. Even very young babies can demonstrate that they also prefer to be with a particular key person rather than another.

Practical activities

- Build up a collection of songs and rhymes about fingers and toes. Search the internet to add variety to your repertoire. Take photographs of the babies joining in with the actions and display or give to parents/carers so that they can use them at home.

- Provide a collection of mats with interesting surface textures such as furry, cork and bamboo. Help and support babies to explore these by demonstrating with your bare feet so they can see you also have toes like theirs.

- Say the rhyme 'Here is your face and here is your nose, here are your fingers and here are your toes' in front of a mirror, pointing to each part as you say it. Then change the word 'your' to 'my' and repeat the rhyme.

- Babies enjoy eating with their fingers; this also gives them a sense of power and control. Select a variety of suitable foods for them to enjoy this experience.

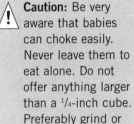

Caution: Be very aware that babies can choke easily. Never leave them to eat alone. Do not offer anything larger than a $\frac{1}{4}$-inch cube. Preferably grind or chop food.

Toddlers

Keen observations help practitioners plan for children's individual differences, their strengths and interests. Although there are recognisable developmental stages that practitioners need to cater for it is essential not to use a 'one size fits all' approach. Children's growth and development comes in spurts and lulls. Their individual growth patterns are dependent on hereditary and environmental factors. It is important not to compare children's achievement, even those from the same family, but to recognise and celebrate each child's own personal qualities, abilities and progress.

Practical activities

- Play body awareness games such as 'Heads, shoulders, etc.', encouraging the children to join in and touch the relevant parts of their body.

- To further body awareness, introduce body massage, yoga and physical development activities (see Resources).

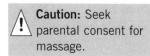

Caution: Seek parental consent for massage.

- Encourage the children to create a happy picture about themselves: 'I am glad to be me'. Talk about their picture and add captions with comments about the things they like, their friends, what they like to be called, their favourite toys. Let them revisit the picture to add details if they wish.

- Create a child-sized puppet or a large two-dimensional picture. Point out the things that all the children have in common: eyes, nose, ears, arms and legs and so on. Use safety mirrors to confirm and compare with a partner/friend. Emphasise the similarities.

- Ask all the children with brown eyes to stand up, followed by those who have curly hair (choose a different characteristic each time). Have a large safety mirror in a central position so they can check for themselves. Include non-physical statements such as 'Stand up if you like ice-cream'. This can help to strengthen children's individuality while contributing to a sense of belonging.

- On admission, take a photograph of each child. During the year capture significant moments and activities on film. At the end of the year, display the children's photographs as a time line, showing how they have changed and the activities they have enjoyed. These can later be transferred into a record of their time in the setting to take home.

Outcomes for the child

- Being able to make choices.
- Being able to show preferences.
- Becoming an individual.

Focus points

It is interesting that identical twins that are physically and psychologically very close differ in their personalities. In some pairs, one will be left-handed and the other right; one tidy and organised, the other not. Although it may be difficult for others to tell identical twins apart, some are able to recognise and identify their twin brother/sister as such when shown a photograph.

Helping children to be strong is complex when dealing with babies and young children. During this period of their life, they are very self-centred and sometimes find it hard to accept that others have needs that are different from, or conflict with, their own. Practitioners need sensitivity and good communication skills. Records require carefully observed individual profiles with evidence to support statements, as reporting to parents/carers demands accuracy.

Staff discussion

- Collect a selection of newspapers and magazines about celebrities and ask staff to try to create a word picture about one of the celebrities. How accurate do they think the media information is? How consistent is it across the different publications? Much of what we know is based on second-hand information and assumptions. Use this to show that when we make judgements about a baby/young child it must be based on real situations and have supporting evidence.
- Staff could consider how they work as a team and have similar goals yet their individual priorities, interests and needs differ.

4. Preferences

Children show their particular characteristics, preferences and interests and demonstrate these in all they do.

(*Birth to Three Matters*)

Babies

In order to show preferences and decisions there must be choice. Babies need some choice but not an overwhelming amount of toys and equipment or opportunities that come in thick and fast. They need time to assimilate what is being offered, to assess what it is. Communicating with babies means focusing on them totally and not partially watching them or talking over them. Babies can use their body language and their facial gestures to make their preferences understood to other babies and adults.

It is helpful to sit alongside a baby when showing her a new activity/resource. Demonstrate and repeat in an encouraging manner in order to capture her interest and to get her to engage.

Practical activities

- Provide a collection of balls for babies – ensure they are small enough for them to hold. Use woven balls, sponge or stress balls, unused, textured dog balls, balls with bells/squeakers. These differently textured balls can help babies with sensory disabilities such as deafness or partial sight and give them the choice and opportunity to have preferences (meeting diverse needs).

- Provide a collection of discovery bottles (small-sized water bottles with interesting items inside). Use some smooth bottles that roll quickly, and some that are made from ribbed plastic. Observe how babies hold and play with the discovery bottles.

- Provide a treasure basket with small items and tools that have handles – spoons, brushes, cups, etc. Observe how babies try to grasp the items and note which ones they can grasp and hold. Notice if they repeatedly choose the same items.

Toddlers

Young children develop their individual preferences, their likes and dislikes, as a result of emotional feedback from previous experiences. If these were good and gave them a sensation of pleasure or satisfaction, they will want to repeat the experiences. If on the other hand they felt a sense of failure, hurt, frustration or anxiety, they will not be motivated to repeat them. It is the fusion of a range of different experiences and emotions that helps to make each of us into an individual. Sometimes making a decision involves taking a risk, accepting a challenge, doing something in a new or different way, and in order to do this young children have to feel good about themselves and have confidence in their ability.

Practical activities

- Create some simple rules for use in the setting. Keep them brief, few in number and positive, for example 'Play safely', 'Be friendly', 'Share' rather than 'Don't . . .', or 'Danger'. Discuss the rules they have at home, for example 'Don't run across the road', 'Clean your teeth before going to bed/watching TV'. Do they know the reason behind the rule – the why? Establish the need for safety and thinking of others. Display the rules with simple pictures, drawn by the children, to illustrate and remind them. Refer to the rules when beginning free play and be consistent. If appropriate, talk about the possible consequences of acting selfishly or thoughtlessly.

- During Circle Time talk about the choices available; make sure they know what is on offer, where to find resources and the rules (as above). In this way the children will have time to consider their choices and feelings of anxiety are lessened.

- Too many choices and too much freedom can overwhelm a young child or toddler. Limit to a choice of alternatives – this one or that: sand or water; inside or outside, quiet, reflective activities or active and physical play.

- Be aware that children will be at different stages and provide for differentiation. For example, some may just want to experience the feel of the sand, play with it, run it through their fingers, while others will be ready for more thought-provoking problem solving and will need challenging resources: tubes, tunnels, pipes, ramps.

- Let the children dress up and if they wish wear the chosen clothes all day.

- Organise snack time as a café, so the children decide when they get food and drink. Have a menu with pictures of alternatives and encourage each child to make a choice.

Outcomes for the child

- Having choice and making choices.
- Having early experiences of making simple decisions.
- Being able to be an individual with some power over their world.
- Understanding that our actions affect others.

Focus points

During a session the activities may be divided into structured play, planned by the adult to develop specific skills, and spontaneous play, when the children make their own choices. Yet even here, the adult has already made a number of decisions: the availability of equipment and resources, time, space and safety. By the careful observation of children's needs and interests, practitioners can offer choices that provide good opportunities for success, and reinforce with praise and encouragement for independent decision making. Even though the children are given the freedom to make choices and communicate their likes and dislikes it is important that they have the security of the presence of a familiar, supportive adult.

Staff discussion

- Babies can show preferences by turning away, closing their lips (if they do not want any more food). List the different ways that you have observed. Have a focus week when all staff sharpen their awareness of how babies show their preferences.

- What choices do babies/young children have in their day? Their reliance on adults is high when they are babies, less so for toddlers. Although most of their choices will be centred on play, how much autonomy do they have over other decisions?

- Preferences are based on experiences – how rich are the experiences that you offer babies and toddlers on a daily basis?

- By careful observation you can obtain a clearer idea of how babies demonstrate their preferences. If necessary, revise the current observational sheets for the baby room, as this is a specialist area and needs a tailored observation sheet.

- How do you organise for babies and young children to have genuine opportunities to make choices and show their preferences? What strategies, resources, staffing need to be in place? How do you prepare the children to become autonomous?

5. Strengths

Plan activities to allow children to show what they can do...
(Birth to Three Matters)

Babies

Babies love having eye contact with their carers and parents; it means they are getting the positive response of full attention. Some children, who may have special needs, find it difficult to hold or to maintain eye contact, so non-engagement might be an early warning signal; however, this is only one factor to consider. It is felt that babies respond to their mother's eyes from the moment of birth and by six weeks will instinctively smile at black geometric spots. Smiling decreases when adult eye contact is removed. These interactions become the early development of a 'conversation'. Positive reinforcements help to build a sense of trust that strengthens the formation of social relationships, giving self-awareness and the knowledge that they have the power to influence others.

Practical activities

- Tummy time. Baby and carer lie on their tummies facing each other, spend time 'talking' to each other and playing with toys.
- Hold baby facing you and sing a simple song using different voices, changing from high to low. If the baby tries to copy you, give smiles and cuddles.

- When baby is in a buggy, position yourself opposite her and engage in full eye contact. Use a soft voice to tell her how clever she is, how lovely. Take time to listen when she begins to experiment with language and give positive responses such as smiles and nods.

- Through careful observation, learn what will distract a baby from a negative feeling into a good feeling. For example, if a baby is distressed, will she respond to a favourite toy, music, rocking, or snuggles?

Toddlers

Toddlers and young children have to try to do things for the very first time, so it is important that their attempts are supported well and their achievements celebrated. This includes their efforts to relate to others and, depending on the responses they receive, influences their personalities and behaviours in positive or negative ways. If they encounter frustration and failure or are not given enough time to 'have a go' for themselves, they may give up, feeling useless or rejected. Children with high self-esteem are willing to try new things, they are able to work on their own initiative and have a good awareness of their strengths and weaknesses. They are willing to ask for help when they need it. Those who have low self-esteem will destroy their work, put off doing it, not finish or say 'I'm bored', flitting from one activity to another. They need the security of a significant adult who they can trust and who gives them constant reassurance and encouragement.

Practical activities

- Create a 'Can do' flower that is coloured in to show when each child has made a particular achievement. These can be differentiated to match individual children's abilities. For example, one toddler might have good personal independence, such as being able to dress, wash hands or tie shoelaces without help and this is celebrated and recognised; another child may need support and time but eventually learns to drink from a cup without spilling.

- Prepare badges, with an appropriate picture/symbol that says 'I can'. Take photographs of the achievement and keep in an 'I can' book. Add simple text, name and date. Celebrate and share with parents/carers.

- Encourage the children to have a 'can do' mentality. Use positive words such as: 'You can', You are good at . . . ', 'You could . . . ',' You like . . . '

- Make a time line that shows each child's significant moments since coming to the setting.

- During Circle Time pass a smile to a friend and say something kind/positive about them. In the beginning their comments may be simply about physical or material things: 'I like Aisha's shoes', but with coaching they will begin to look for personality qualities: 'She is my friend, she is kind and shares with me'.
- Demonstrate how to use a mobile or telephone to make a pretend call and tell them of an achievement: 'You will never guess what I did today!'
- Use a suitable display board to celebrate items such as 'Good News'.
- At the close of the session, ask the children to recall the good things they have done so that they leave the setting with a positive feeling.

Outcomes for the child

- Increased self-confidence and self-worth.
- Willingness to try new experiences.
- Feeling valued.
- Able to make secure relationships with others.

Focus points

Strengths and weaknesses (mastery and helplessness) are not related to intelligence but are connected to the view we have of ourselves. It is the deep-rooted belief we have created, often mistakenly, in our capacity to achieve. These feelings are formed in early childhood and are shaped by how we think others see us and value us. This can influence our achievements and our relationships for the rest of our lives.

Some children may receive as many as 400 negative statements in a day, reinforcing their own poor self-image. Throughout a child's years at school, this could amount to thousands of criticisms. However, any praise needs to be genuine, identifying what they have done well and encouraging further development. For example, when a carer is presented with a painting, an example of empty praise would be to say 'Oh boy! That's great/fantastic/marvellous' and then put the painting on a shelf without a second glance. A more specific and constructive responsive would be to say 'I really like this picture. You have used bright colours and shapes. Next time you could...'

Staff discussion

- Initial early years training gives very little information about eye contact or the influence of direct gaze. Encourage staff awareness. Know that in some cultures direct eye contact is avoided, the gaze is lowered.

- Do staff give children unhurried time to try to do things for themselves such as putting on an apron/coat/shoes? They will need support in the beginning but rushing in and doing it for them undermines their ability to do it for themselves.

- Are there ways that the staff team can celebrate their own successes?

- As a team discuss areas where you feel inadequate and where that feeling came from, for example 'I can't sing/draw/play sports'. Look at these feelings positively – you can't at the moment but what if you could? Would you like to be able to do this?

6. Diverse needs

Babies develop an understanding and awareness of themselves, which is influenced by their family, culture, other people and the environment.

(*Birth to Three Matters*)

Babies

Every baby develops her own individual characteristics and personality. This is determined by aspects inherited from her parents, her family environment and also by the events in her life. Adults within a baby's environment have a significant effect upon the care and nurture they offer the infant who is totally reliant on those who care for her. A strong cultural identity really helps a baby to develop a positive and definite view of herself.

Practical activities

- Collect a range of photographs for each baby that shows who they are and where they come from. Laminate these to use with the baby, not as a record in the office. Secure onto a key ring tab together with the baby's first name. The first photo should be of the baby. Look at them with the baby, adding new photos as appropriate.
- Make up a basket with items that reflect a baby's family life such as small balti dishes, fabrics and familiar items. Enlist the help of parents/carers to discover what is special to their baby.
- Use coffee or cocoa to colour the dough for creating more realistic skin colours.
- Use mangoes or yams to roll instead of plastic balls.
- Check the pictures in baby books to ensure that they show a range of cultures and positive role models.
- Cover sleep mattresses or physical exercise mats with ethnic cloths/saris to make a colourful mat to crawl along.
- Have a dolls and teddy bears' picnic with ethnic cookware as well as the traditional tea set. Dress them in a variety of clothing – creating an exotic, multicultural picnic.

Toddlers

Toddlers and young children want to be accepted by their peers and carers – to fit in. Rejection at any age is cruel and difficult to deal with, more so when you are just finding out about your self. Children need to understand that differences are normal, even within a family, and that no two people are identical – they don't have the same likes and dislikes, don't all do the same things at the same time. Even within an all-white community there will be differences of culture and lifestyle.

Practical activities

- Welcome each child and parent/carer. If their mother tongue is not English, find out the words they use for a simple greeting and use them.

- Create activities/role-play scenarios that start from the known and the familiar. Later these can be developed to include the wider world. Help the children to discover features of their local environment, for example if it's a rural location, provide farm toys, animals and vehicles that they know. Create scenarios that reflect familiar everyday experiences or the jobs that parents/carers do. Talk about individual experiences and show how we all have different likes, dislikes (see section 3, 'Similarities and differences', above).

- Include multicultural play people in small world resources. Collect artefacts and items, pictures, photos, costumes, music that will be familiar and incorporate into the resources. Read dual language books (see Resources).

- Search for videos and stories that have prejudice or diversity as a theme, for example *Pingu and the Strangers* (video) and Arnold Sundgaard's story of *The Lamb and the Butterfly* and use them to initiate a discussion about feelings.

- Help young children to explore and accept new and different experiences such as providing a range of food at snack time that comes from different parts of the world.

Outcomes for the child

- Developing respect for others.
- Learning to accept differences by widening experiences.
- Developing confidence and self-worth.
- Awareness of being an individual.
- Feeling part of the environment.

Focus points

We live in a multicultural society which includes people from many different races, religions and countries of origin. This has caused a dynamic change to the traditional British way of life, enriching and enhancing it. Many aspects of other cultures have become so subtly woven into our lifestyles that we are no longer aware of their origins.

Culture is the learned behaviour that is passed on from adults to children. Some children adapt and learn to live in two different cultures – home and school; others may find it difficult. Religion influences culture by providing a set of rules, ways to worship, special diet and dress codes. Ethnicity is not just about colour and each ethnic group brings with it its own particular lifestyle and this has also contributed to social change.

One of our basic instincts is to reject or fear what we don't understand. It can be unsettling to discover that everything we believe in and know is different from someone else's experiences. Practitioners need to help young children deal with these confusing concepts by encouraging them to understand that different is not better, or worse, just different.

Staff discussion

- Encourage staff that do not live in the area where they work to take time to visit the local environment. Observe the street life, its colours, sounds and smells, the people, shops and traffic.
- Think about the things we take for granted that have come from elsewhere – food, vocabulary, clothes, music, literature, films (think Disney, USA).
- Be aware that children come to the setting with many different family experiences and expectations.
- Babies and young children are experts at interpreting gestures and body language; they are able to read your attitudes and values through subtle changes. They can tell a real smile and a warm welcome from a fake one.
- It is the everyday life in the setting that promotes equal opportunities rather than one-off special festival days. However, if you do celebrate multicultural festivals, check with parents/carers beforehand that what you will be doing is correct. Try to visit the local religious centres to understand that part of the children's lives. Research beforehand what to wear and how to behave so as not to unwittingly offend.
- Developing a good self-image is central to equal opportunity, whatever race, religion or colour you are. It is important for practitioners to strengthen children's respect for their own identity and to accept others'. Discuss as a staff team some of the ways this can be achieved.

References

Ball, C. (1994) *Start Right: The Importance of Early Learning*. London: RSA.

DfES (Department for Education and Skills) (2002) *Birth to Three Matters: A Framework to Support Children in their Earliest Years*. London: DfES.

DfES (Department for Education and Skills) (2003) *Every Child Matters*. London: DfES.

DfES (Department for Education and Skills)/DWP (Department for Work and Pensions) (2003) *National Standards for Under 8s Day Care and Childminding (Full Day Care)*. London: DfES.

Postle, D. (1989) *The Mind Gymnasium*. London: Macmillan.

Resources

Specialist children's massage programmes and trained instructors can be found by contacting the International Association of Infant Massage at www.iaim.org.uk and at www.bodybasiconline.co.uk

The British Wheel of Yoga website can be found at www.bwy.org.uk

Action Kids: A Healthy Child by Ann Roberts and Val Sabin (Val Sabin Publications, 2006) can be obtained through info@valsabinpublications.com

Staff background reading:

● *For Every Child* edited by Caroline Castle (Red Fox, 2002)

● 'Pingu' story books and videos

● *Frog and the Stranger* by Max Velthuijs (Anderson Press, 2005)

A discussion forum about dual language children – www.multilingualchildren.org

Publishers who have a range of dual language books and cultural stories – www.milet.com

Check out the selection of stories from Random House Publishers that deal with personal, social and emotional aspects, such as:

● *Elmer the Elephant* by David Mckee, 1990 (Being different)

● *The Mixed-Up Chameleon* by Eric Carle, 1975 (Being oneself)

● *The Lamb and the Butterfly* by Arnold Sundgaard, 1988 (Diversity)

● *Dogger* by Shirley Hughes, 1977 (Family life and kindness)

Note

'Equal opportunity is the right of the individual no matter what race, gender, intellectual ability, health or religion'. The Race Relations Act 1976 makes racial discrimination unlawful in education, employment and in the provision of childcare.

2 A sense of belonging

Introduction

Emotional intelligence matters more than IQ.

(Goleman, 1996)

For the first months of life a mother and baby tune in to each other's rhythms; they develop a synchrony whereby their breathing and body language are in tune. When babies or young children are placed in day care their senses are suddenly confronted with a whole range of different sights, sounds, smells, tastes, touches and people. It is not surprising that they may squirm, stiffen and cry as they experience strange feelings, emotions and insecurities. Practitioners have the difficult task of taking on board babies, each one with unique attributes and needs, and helping them to settle, to trust them and to form close attachments with them.

When a young child/toddler enters a setting, he is at an important stage of personal, social and emotional development, a time when he is developing an emerging sense of self, finding out how he fits into the world and how others respond to him. The feedback he receives can affect how he views himself, his level of confidence and his ability to form positive relationships. It is not surprising that strong emotions may erupt so that this critical period is known as 'the terrible twos'. The practitioners' role is all-important and has a strong impact on how well a child feels he belongs. They have to immediately establish a positive rapport that will cement a child's social confidence and self-management. There is a delicate balance on intervening at a time when a young child/toddler, eager to become independent and assert his identity, lacks many of the necessary social and intellectual skills. Adults have to stand back, be patient and wait before jumping in and taking over. Simple coaching techniques together with practical activities can help to develop a child's self-confidence and self-management skills and his personal, social and emotional growth. Regularly celebrating successes with genuine praise and recognition and then sharing these with parents/carers helps children to know that they are 'doing OK'. Relationships will be different between each child and each adult and some pairings may prove difficult to maintain. But each child needs to feel loved, be accepted unconditionally and welcomed and to be part of the group. With the right nurturing, the child has the chance to develop into a strong and stable individual.

1. Snuggling

'Snuggling in' gives young babies physical, psychological and emotional comfort.

(*Birth to Three Matters*)

Babies

According to a number of scientists, cuddling babies provides them with many benefits that help to develop positive social behaviour. They found a clear link between love and attention in the early years and healthy emotional responses in later life. Researchers found that those children who have been deprived of physical contact as babies have lower levels of social-bonding hormones. Even when smothered with love as toddlers, without this early bonding, it is hard to repair the damage that has been done to their social competence. The research, published in the Journal Proceedings of the National Academy of Sciences, looked at the levels of hormones called oxytocin and arginine vasopressin. These both play an important role in the body's response to stress and social bonding. After a child has been comforted through human contact, the levels of both of these hormones rise in the brain and induce the effect of bonding and well-being.

Practical activities

- Create an area in the setting known as the 'snuggle' zone. Use soft textiles, cushioning and comfortable flooring. Decorate with photographs of babies from all walks of life being cuddled. This will encourage and raise awareness of the importance of cuddles. This is not to say that you should only cuddle babies in this area.

- Accept that babies will wish to have comforters to cuddle as well as people, soft toys, and fabric and special items from home. Have an extra selection available.

- Welcome babies with a cuddle and say 'bye bye' with a smile and a wave. Take photos of greetings and display them, giving the message that snuggles are important.

- If babies are unsettled, they may need to be swaddled; wrapped in a blanket, and gently rocked into a more relaxed state.

Toddlers

At times young children and toddlers will still seek a snuggle/cuddle, in particular when they are upset, hurt or distressed. As they mature, their need for closeness is shown in other ways. They look for acceptance, approval and want to be recognised as an individual – needs which represent a form of psychological closeness. Feeling secure in their environment and developing trust with the people who care for them is crucial.

Practical activities

- Define a special area for telling stories or for one-to-one talking times. Have a low chair, such as a nursing chair, for the storyteller and comfortable cushions for the children to curl up on. Some children may want to get very close at these times and lean against the adult or climb up on her knee.

- Create play opportunities when the staff get to be at the children's level, playing alongside them on the floor, sharing in their problem solving and creative play.

- Talk regular walks outside with the children. Some toddlers will take this opportunity for a feeling of closeness and want to hold the adult's hand.

- Giving genuine praise and encouragement helps develop a young child's view of self, how he measures up and develops a sense of pride and satisfaction.

- Play collaborative games where children have a partner, such as 'Michael row the boat', holding hands and rocking backwards and forwards.

- Create a project where a small group has to work co-operatively, for example washing something big together, being involved in creating a garden, digging, planting, moving soil, joining up as a team to have a pretend car wash. Ask the children for suggestions. Listen carefully as they engage in problem solving and co-operating.

- Play 'Copy cat' with a small group by subtly mirroring their body language, facial expressions and breathing pattern. This mirroring and matching can create synchrony and a feeling of belonging.

- Help young children to learn to relate to a wider group of adults. If their key person is absent, ensure they know who to turn to. Increase the opportunities for the children to build up relationships with a wider group of adults: other key workers, assistants, admin. staff, voluntary helpers.

  > ⚠ **Caution:** Be aware of the Code of Practice and CRB (Criminal Records Bureau) rules.

- Create strong links with home: encourage the children to share their news; have a special place where they can keep their treasures; let parents/carers know the positive things they have achieved.

Outcomes for the child

- Feeling secure and wanted.
- Feeling welcome.
- Feeling part of the group.
- Feeling accepted.

Focus points

In the animal kingdom to be rejected by the pack means lack of food, shelter and projection – a life-threatening situation. In our human society, it remains a basic need to be accepted by the group, to belong. The feeling of rejection is very distressing for a baby or toddler. Sometimes it happens that the key person and the child do not develop a good rapport and the child is very quick to sense it. In these cases, it is beneficial to change the pairing. Being close and being touched is reassuring and necessary yet in the interests of child protection, we must always be aware of what is appropriate.

It is up to the adult carer to make babies and young children feel safe and secure in knowing that the adult can be trusted.

Staff discussion

- Look for ways to develop listening skills. What are the signals you give to children that say you are really paying attention, are genuinely interested in what they are saying?

- Consider infant carriers, where the baby is supported close to the body in a sling and the practitioner is able to move around the environment. These are used by parents/carers in many parts of the world.

- Consider the question in *Birth to Three Matters*: 'do you only give a cuddle in response to a baby's needs?' Look at your written policies, the National Standards and how you respond to a baby's well-being.

- How proactive are the staff of the baby room in giving cuddles? Do they give the same amount of attention to each baby?

- Observe staff and note the level of closeness they achieve in the baby room. Talk with them one to one and discuss if there are any areas of development. Use a more experienced practitioner to encourage young or less experienced staff.

- Develop an information sheet for parents/carers on the importance of bonding and closeness for babies and young children. Be aware that some cultures may have their own codes of parent/child behaviour.

- Build strong partnerships with parents. Arrange for families and staff to meet informally, with and without the children, such as at coffee mornings, afternoon tea, trips or picnics.

2. Trust

To sustain healthy emotional attachments babies need familiar, trusting, safe and secure relationships.

(*Birth to Three Matters*)

Babies

Being close and having healthy emotional attachments actually helps babies to feel comforted, calm and reassured. In full day care this is often the role of the key person – the adult who is allocated to look after each baby, keep their records and communicate regularly with parents, especially about the babies' daily progress and well-being. Healthy attachments mean maintaining a consistently professional approach. Parents and carers may really want to look after their babies themselves but for many different reasons cannot do this full time. This can be an emotional period for them so the professional practitioner needs to keep this in mind and show sensitivity when sharing a baby's special moments with parents/carers.

Practical activities

● Have a bubbles and cuddles time – water play session with baby. As you dry her sing songs and rhymes, wrap her securely in a towel and give her a cuddle.

● Wiggle, giggle and dance. Spend time with an individual baby, ensuring that the relationship you have develops. Having fun and laughing together ensures a feel good factor.

● Share books that mention cuddles, for example Dorling Kindersley baby board books including *I Like*.

Toddlers

As a toddler develops an emerging sense of self, finds his feet, his voice and his mind, he will be experiencing a range of emotions, sometimes needing a close attachment and at other times wanting to go off on his own and explore further afield. There needs to be safe opportunities for him to try out this independence yet have the security of the knowledge that a familiar adult is close by. During this time, he may want to take control of everything the adult used to do for him, although not yet fully competent. He will need support and encouragement even if it is simply a reassuring smile, a nod or a 'Hmm' and sometimes the suggestion 'Let's try doing this together'. Practitioners also need to show that they take a young child's fears, concerns and worries seriously, make time to listen carefully and respond in the best way they can.

Practical activities

● Security comes from the knowledge that the environment is stable and predictable. Establish daily patterns and routines and simple boundaries. At

Circle Time talk about what will be happening during the day, what is on offer, where activities and adults can be found. Be consistent in the use of simple rules, boundaries and limits. In this way, the children will know what is expected and what is allowed. Some boundaries will have to be made by adults for safety reasons, although some can be agreed with the children.

- Address strong emotions; don't ignore them or brush them aside. They are very real to the young child, who may get upset or distressed. Talk about what has happened and try to find ways to address the immediate situation. Tell the child you understand that he is feeling hurt/angry/sad, and give him time and space to calm down. Then suggest a toy/book/friend to play with until he feels better.

- Use life-sized puppets or large cartoon-type pictures, to help the children develop their social awareness and understanding of others. Address specific behaviours by making up simple, comical stories and defining characters such as Saeed 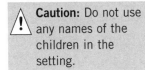 **Caution:** Do not use any names of the children in the setting.

Selfish, Willy Want, Gertie Grumble or Charlie Cheerful. Ask the children what they liked or disliked about the characters.

- Take an active part in the children's games, pretend play or dancing with them. In this way you can actively help the shy or reticent child to join in with the group.

Outcomes for the child

- Developing trusting relationships.
- Feeling safe and secure.
- Knowledge that adults care about them.

Focus points

Be aware that some children may have several different carers during the day/week. Each one of these situations may have a different philosophy, set of rules, boundaries and expectations. Each may put a different emphasis on what he does. This is confusing and distressing for a child. Try to establish what children experience in the settings or with the carers and create links to their time with you.

Staff discussion

- Look for ways to manage staff time so that each member of the team can spend quality one-to-one time with babies and young children.

- Discuss what is appropriate/inappropriate behaviour in forming close attachments and establish acceptable guidelines.

- As toddlers and young children develop their sense of self and gain independence they will demonstrate a wide range of behaviours and experience a range of conflicting emotions. Staff need to recognise this while accepting the children unconditionally.

- Some babies and young children are very difficult to get close to. This may be down to their individual personalities or deeper emotional issues. Staff need to be aware of this, make careful observations and if concerned, seek specialist help from outside agencies.

- Look to find ways of employing simple coaching techniques that will help to resolve conflicts and move negative situations forward.

3. Well-being

Note the ways you nurture babies' sense of themselves whilst also helping them feel they belong to the group.

(Birth to Three Matters)

Babies

In order to support babies by nurturing a sense of self, practitioners need to respect their feelings and encourage them to make individual choices. The effective organisation of the environment, routines and ways of doing things helps to make it a place where babies feel safe and are able to be themselves. The practitioner has a key role in helping a baby develop a sense of belonging and being part of the group. Through careful observation, watching, looking and listening, the adult can build a picture of each baby's developing sense of self. This is highlighted in the *Birth to Three Matters* guidelines.

Practical activities

- Focus on each baby's name and use it often throughout the day. If the name is unusual or difficult to pronounce, ask parents/carers to help. Write it phonetically to help you say it correctly.

- Insert babies' name into songs, rhymes, lullabies and simple stories. Their name is an important part of a sense of self.

- Focus your attention fully when engaging with a baby. Let the baby take the lead and then imitate her. Avoid hurrying or snatching moments to communicate with a baby – make it quality time. Try to avoid distractions such as talking to other adults over a baby's head.

- Begin to build up a profile of the baby, including her preferences, favourite toys and sleep patterns. Try to discover who or what is important to each child. It may be a pet, a toy, a sibling, a grandparent. Inject these into activities. This needs to be done through close co-operation with parents/carers. Discover their weekend activities, places they go on holidays. Make it clear to the parents/carers how this can help their child; discuss in a professional way, without being intrusive.

Toddlers

To enhance a toddler's feeling of well-being he needs to know that he is accepted and is special to his significant people. With feelings of security and trust he knows that he can rely on them to meet his basic needs: safety, relief of pain, hunger, tiredness. However, well-being is also developed through the pleasure of receiving positive words and gestures. These reinforce the feeling of being liked and being good at things.

Circle Time is a good opportunity for helping children to feel connected with each other and see themselves as part of the whole group. The idea of Circle Time has been around for 200 years (Friedrich Froebel) and there are many different activities that can be used successfully to support well-being.

Practical activities

- Create a circle and pass a smile. Catch the children being good and at Circle Time give them genuine compliments, for example 'Sarah, you were very good today sharing your teddy with Malik'. Start a game of Chinese Whispers, where each child passes on a message.

- Provide a goody bag with sparkly items, soft and textured fabrics, holographic paper and encourage each child to make his own 'Identity' card. This can be used on his coat peg or special treasure box.

- Have fun with face paints – adults and children together.

- Play parachute games where the children collaborate by holding the parachute, lifting it high then low, trying to run under it one by one or rolling a ball around its surface.

- Provide strips of fabric, ribbons, string and a large branch from a tree. Remove all the leaves and knobbly bits. Let the children decorate the branch or weave the materials to create a large communal work of art.

- Arrange a tea party (coffee morning) for parents and carers. Let the children be in control, setting the table, arranging flowers and playing host/hostess.

- Recognise and celebrate special days. These will usually be birthdays but other times might be appropriate such as the birth of a brother/sister or a special achievement. Dress up and have a parade, playing musical instruments and singing songs.

Outcomes for the child

- Increased levels of self-esteem.
- Feeling valued.
- A sense of belonging.

Focus points

An early childcare setting is like a small community and all the children and people in it rely on each other. At times, it can be stressful for all concerned: relationships become strained and the work/life balance is upset. Take time to stand back and reflect on what it is like for the babies and toddlers in the setting. For some they have only just started to explore the wider world and have been standing on their own two unsteady feet for a few months. It is the only time in their life when they can enjoy being two or three years old. Think about the ways that you as a practitioner can make this the best time of their life.

Staff discussion

- Being an effective observer means acquiring finely tuned skills, especially with non-verbal babies. Being reflective and thinking in a more diagnostic way about what to do next, also requires sensitivity and efficient time management. Check which staff would benefit from further professional development in these areas. Examine programmes such as the Effective Early Learning programme for guidance (see Resources).

- Construct an annual programme for improving communication with parents and look for ways to develop a strong, mutual partnership, improving knowledge of languages and an awareness of cultural/ethnic beliefs.

- Be aware that members of staff may have strong biases, make value judgements and bring personal preferences and beliefs to the setting and these can affect how they interact with children.

- How do staff react to a toddler who has not yet mastered toileting skills? Are mishaps handled sensitively, without causing embarrassment or shame?

- How does the setting consider the well-being of the staff? Are there areas that can be improved?

4. Space

Provide each child with their own place in which to keep their own things. This nurtures a sense of belonging.

(*Birth to Three Matters*)

Babies

Coming from home into a new environment means the baby has to settle in and build a sense of belonging to that new space. The environment, people and the ethos all play their part. Bridging the gap can be made easier when staff form a close relationship with parents and carers. The babies will still need their comforters, their special feed/cups/bottles or nappies and creams. A baby gets used to the type of nappies and creams her parents/carers use and is uncomfortable and sensitive to change. Catering for these physical needs are essential for the baby's well-being. If these basics are addressed, then a sense of belonging can be built more easily.

Practical activities

- Have easily identifiable containers for babies' nappy-changing requirements; label them with a photograph as well as their name. This helps parents/carers see where to put personal items and also reassures them that their baby is being treated as an individual.

- The coat/bag area should be baby friendly, not like a reception class cloakroom. Create a collage of the faces of all the babies in the group together with their key persons. Label pegs/containers with names and photos and keep them up to date as the baby grows.

- Use open-fronted units for boxes containing treasured items/toys with the baby's photo at the back of the unit.

Toddlers

Good organisation is important in helping a young child establish a sense of well-being. Many get upset when things change. As they develop their independence, it helps if they know where to find toys, resources and equipment. Likewise if they know and understand the routines of the day and the expectations for good behaviour, it gives them enough of a secure structure to feel comfortable in their environment.

Practical activities

- When preparing for activities encourage the children to get engaged in setting them up. Play a game of 'I spy' that helps children to locate resources and be aware of where to find them and also where to return them. Give simple descriptions such as 'I am looking for a brush with a very long handle', or 'I spy a big box of bricks; who can find it for me?'

- Organise the room into clearly defined zones, using low furniture, screens or floor carpet/tiles to separate areas. Have photos of children playing with the sand/water together with labels and symbols that identify the activity. Make sure the children are aware of what these mean. Refer to them during the day.

- To encourage independence have resources in low units, accessible and easy-to-lift, clear containers, or if using boxes, label these with symbols and photos of the content.

- Create a special area where you and the children can display their treasures, models or pictures. Label with names and/or photos. Make sure parents/carers are aware of this 'Gallery' and encourage them to look at the items. Make positive comments about them in front of the child, for example 'Luke worked very hard today to make this model. He has used lots of different materials in an interesting way.'

Outcomes for the child

- When parents/carers are happy with the provision, their calmness is transmitted to the child.

- Children understand that their special items are welcomed and that they are too.

- A well-organised environment helps a child to feel secure.

Focus points

When setting up a room it can be difficult to strike a balance between clutter, chaos, muddle and a barren, sterile, over-structured environment. Babies and toddlers need stimulation, interesting items, areas where they can make a mess, things to explore and places for a quiet snuggle. How can this all fit into the available space? If a visitor came, what would be his/her first impression? If supply staff had to work in the room, how easily would they find things? Start by trying to see the area from the child's point of view. Get down low; what can you see, touch or feel? Examine individual items and think about why you have chosen them, what impact will they have on a baby/toddler? Ask yourself who the environment is for and what is its purpose? The answers may help you assess what is important and what can be rejected or stored for the future. Aim to make an area of the floor that is clear and can have a multitude of uses and where children can crawl, play or walk safely. Hopefully, the environment will appear brighter, lighter and more spacious.

Staff discussion

- What do you do to make babies/toddlers feel they are welcome and belong? How can positive messages be communicated to parents/carers that they and their children are welcome and belong?

- How can you use photographs effectively as opposed to text to send messages to parents and carers, especially in a multicultural environment?

- Encourage staff to develop their digital camera skills and knowledge of IT (information technology) to facilitate communication, record learning and stages of development.

- Make an inventory of resources; discard items that are broken, have parts missing, are out of date or unsuitable for the age range.

5. Language

Help children from a family whose first language is not English to gain a sense of belonging within what might seem a strange and unfamiliar context; e.g. by learning how to say 'hello' in a child's home language.

(*Birth to Three Matters*)

Babies

Many babies are brought up in an environment where several languages are spoken. They are treasured beings who are included in family and religious events, celebrations and festivals. Babies appear to be comfortable and able to respond to the different sounds and tones of family language without generally suffering from speech delays. Each culture brings with it richness and diversity and provides an opportunity for practitioners to extend their own skills and expertise. When people travel abroad, the first words they learn of a foreign language are usually 'Hello' and 'Goodbye', their own names and words associated with food and drink. It is helpful if practitioners try to learn these words from each baby's family language.

Practical activities

- As part of the induction or welcome programme, make a note of the languages spoken in the household and the parental wishes linked to these. Have a 'Welcome' board with appropriate forms of greetings. Ensure that this is supported with inclusive pictures of people linked to that culture. Many cultures use gestures when greeting. Try to discover these as well.

- Mealtimes are a time when babies may use dual sounds or languages and so develop the knowledge of key words for items such as milk, water, hungry and more.

- Investigate using universal sign language to communicate with babies.

Toddlers

With increasing migration of families, many young children and toddlers arrive in this country to experience childcare for the very first time. It can be particularly distressing, even frightening, to have to leave the security of the family even for a few hours and enter a strange environment where everyone speaks another language. Some young children try so hard to 'fit in' that they may openly reject their family background and traditions. However, it is up to the practitioner to help the child adjust and maintain positive feelings for family and culture.

Practical activities

- Find out from families some of their traditional songs and rhymes and introduce these in the setting. It will give a sense of pride and respect to the child. The other children will enjoy them even if they don't understand the words.

- Develop a wide range of picture story books and audiotapes from dual language publishers (see Resources). Can the children work out what is happening in the story from the pictures?

- Encourage the children to create their own picture/story books. Use a digital camera and children's own photographs to tell simple stories. These may be based on traditional tales or simple accounts of their own day in the setting.

- Seek out second language storytellers who can visit and tell stories to the children.

- Look for special music/dances for carnivals and festivals, costumes or traditional practices such as henna hand painting. Introduce these into activities.

Outcomes for the child

- The baby/child sees the setting as an extension of the family home.
- A sense of belonging is achieved.
- Being part of a multicultural family can be part of a celebration of themselves.
- Developing a positive identity and a place within the group.

Focus points

Due to economic migration, settings are now admitting a wider range of children from different ethnic and cultural backgrounds than ever before. Helping a child to adjust to a new and strange environment is especially relevant if he is the only one from that culture, for example Eastern European or even British Romany. It may be difficult to obtain resources and this is where the family can assist. It is important that the child feels he has something positive to bring and share with the other children and that his peers accept him unconditionally. Practitioners should seek support from the Local Authority to help them locate foreign language specialists so that they can communicate effectively with parents/carers and families.

Staff discussion

- Fostering staff knowledge, understanding and sensitivity towards other family backgrounds will help to avoid major blunders or upsets to the family and the baby/child. Parents and carers are often proud and pleased to share information if approached in the right way.

- Hold parents' evenings/afternoons which display to parents/carers an appreciation of their cultures. This can be shown by the food prepared, the timing of the event, the attitude, openness and welcome of the staff.

6. Comforting the senses

Provide experiences that involve using all the senses, such as relaxing music, soft lighting and pleasant smells for babies to enjoy.

(*Birth to Three Matters*)

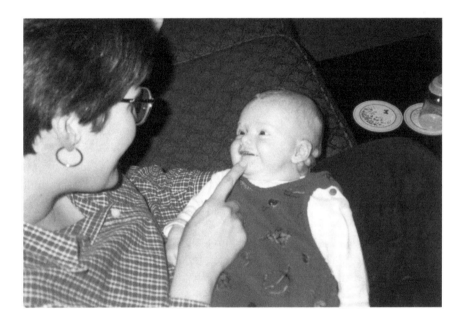

 Babies

Seeing people and things that appeal and respond to us, hearing sounds that make us feel comfortable or assured, tasting things that are familiar and pleasant, touching soft fabrics, feeling calm and cosy and smelling items that are fragrant and pleasing can all give a baby a feeling of comfort, well-being and belonging. Consider how the senses can be stimulated when offering babies play and practical support.

Practical activities

- Lavender can be added to discovery bottles and sprinkled on fabric stress balls. Hang Smelly Teddies (the sort sold as car fresheners) over nappy-changing areas. Place a bowl of pot pourri on a windowsill.

 Caution: Make sure pot pourri is high enough so the babies cannot reach it and put it in their mouth.

- Build up a collection of calming music tapes, including pan pipes and lullabies. Play these at appropriate times such as when putting down to sleep.

- Babies need soft lighting. Very young babies have thin eyelids and benefit from sleeping away from direct sunlight. Down lighters, low wattage or pastel coloured light bulbs also create a sense of calmness. Attach star lights to a branch and suspend over the sleeping area. A sleep area should have a sense of peace. It does not need to be busy with too many displays or brightly coloured pictures.

Toddlers

Although sounds help the development of speech and language, the human voice is the most soothing. Using a quiet and gentle tone can help to calm children. Sight is the main way that children receive information and learn about the world, so it is important that the pictures and symbols you want them to notice are placed within their sightline. Even young babies will make a face to express disgust when given something to eat that they don't like. Toddlers change their acceptance of foods from day to day, sometimes developing an aversion or suddenly taking a liking for a taste. It is worth while waiting and re-presenting a taste, but never force them to eat things they don't want. Food links textures and smells. When food is heated, it releases aromas that send signals to the brain. When selecting fragrances to use in the setting, air fresheners and suchlike, be aware that for some children certain smells can overload the senses and cause nausea.

Caution: Be aware that some oils could cause an adverse reaction to individual children. Check out if any children have breathing problems or allergies that could be triggered by the oils. Take care when handling essential oils as undiluted oils can irritate and even burn the skin.

Practical activities

- Check out the effects of essential oils. Some produce an uplifting feeling while others have a more calming and relaxing effect. For example, chamomile is thought to help calm toddler tantrums! Consider the best diffuser for your needs. You can simply place a few drops on a tissue; however, this produces only a localised effect whereas a water or steam diffuser can disperse the aroma around the room.

- Take the children outside to enjoy the fresh air, the rain on their cheeks, the wind and the sun. Encourage them to take deep breaths; to look up, down, all around; to listen to the small sounds.

- Toddlers enjoy physical movements. Let them jump, hop, spin, skip and run freely.

- Provide different messy play where they can explore sloppy, slimy, bumpy, foamy materials as well as sand, water and mud. Give them experiences of heavy/light, rough/smooth and silky.

- Let them chase and catch bubbles.

Outcomes for the child

- A holistic feeling of well-being and belonging, calm and peace.
- Enjoyment and contentment.
- Connection with the real and natural world.

Focus points

Consider the experiences a baby/toddler has in the setting. What is it like for a baby lying on her tummy or her back for most of the day? Young babies can only see a distance of 9 inches off the ground; do they have a daily view of the skirting board? How can this be improved? Assess how much of a baby's/toddler's world is made up of plastic. Plastic has a very low sensory impact; it does not smell, rarely has textures, and does not taste or have a temperature. What could you use in its place? Think what children would be learning and experiencing if you provided real crockery and utensils in the home play area.

Staff discussion

- How much emphasis is put on providing for the senses when planning activities? Are staff aware of the importance of involving the senses to help develop physical and emotional growth?

- Look for safe ways to incorporate more natural resources and items into your resources and to use with babies and young children.

- Consider how you would tackle a child being called 'smelly'.

References

Alborough, J. (2001) *Hug*. Cambridge, MA: Candlewick.

DfES (Department for Education and Skills) (2002) *Birth to Three Matters: A Framework to Support Children in their Earliest Years*. London: DfES.

DfES (Department for Education and Skills) (2003) *Every Child Matters*. London: DfES.

DfES (Department for Education and Skills)/DWP (Department for Work and Pensions) (2003) *National Standards for Under 8s Day Care and Childminding (Full Day Care)*. London: DfES.

Goleman, D. (1996) *Emotional Intelligence*. London: Bloomsbury.

Katz, K. (2003) *Counting Kisses*. New York: Little Simon.

Resources

Proceedings of the National Academy of Sciences, open access article, 'Early experience effects on social behavior neuropeptides', *PNAS*, 102 (47). Available at www.pnas.org/cgi/content/short/102/47/17237

For information on the Effective Early Learning programme (EEL) contact: The Centre for Research in Early Childhood, St Thomas Centre, Bell Barn Road, Attwood Green, Birmingham B15 2AF. Tel: 0121 464 0020.

For information on multicultural/dual language books, go to:

● www.tamarindbooks.co.uk

● www.letterboxlibrary.com

● www.mantralingua.com

● www.miragetheatre.co.uk for traditional stories told in English and many other languages.

For information on baby signing, visit www.talktoyourbaby.org.uk or read about the Baby Signs Programme at www.babysigns.com

Harpley, A. (2003) *More Play Sense*. London: National Association of Toy and Leisure Libraries (see www.natll.org.uk).

3 Being acknowledged and affirmed

Introduction

This chapter looks at babies' and young children's emotions. The relationships they form with key adults in these early years will shape their lives and decide the kind of adult they will become. Key adults have significant influence and impact so if they get it wrong, there could be long-term negative consequences. It is expected that adult carers will nurture and protect babies and young children. From birth, babies learn to trust that adults will respond to their physical needs so that they can survive. However, their emotional needs are just as important – that is, providing a feeling of security, warmth, closeness and the reassurance that they are lovable. It is how others respond to them and acknowledge them that confirms this. Once a child is taken from his familiar home environment and placed into the hands of strangers (day care) his well-being becomes of prime importance. He may feel distressed, assailed by different smells, sights and sounds and cradled by different arms. However, his resilience is such that he can rapidly learn to form strong attachments with key persons. Carl Rogers (1969) suggests that adults who wish to be effective when working with children should not present a front, a façade but be themselves, be real, sincere and genuine. This produces a ripple of trust, caught by the children, and creates a positive environment, which in turn gives the adult a feeling of satisfaction and a job well done.

As young children mature they develop a whole range of feelings and insecurities, sometimes strong and difficult to control; they become upset and confused. A sensitive and supportive adult can guide a child by helping him to understand these feelings and control them. This chapter focuses on suggesting practical ways of helping a child develop positive feeling about himself. It is also important for staff to examine their own feelings of well-being and self-esteem and know that they too are valued.

1. Seeking attention

Babies seek to gain attention in a variety of ways.

(Birth to Three Matters)

Babies

Understanding how much attention each baby needs can be a complex matter that varies from child to child, with situations and even the time of day. Crying is the main method that a baby uses to seek attention. When the carer is in tune with the baby, she will learn to recognise and differentiate when the crying indicates a physical need, discomfort or hunger. Responding does not always mean carrying and holding the baby. Laying a baby on her tummy and touching or gently rubbing her back lets her know that she is not alone. Ensure babies get a positive response such as eye contact, smiles, cuddles, a wave as well as a reassuring voice. Observe how the baby responds to the attention you give; she may make eye contact, sounds or body movements that show she knows her cries have been acknowledged.

Practical activities

- Set aside a special time where you can have a one-to-one interaction session with your key babies. This allows you to focus on the baby by making contact (smiling, touching and stroking, babbling, pausing and taking turns) and communicating with each other in a physical way. Providing this special time together means that you are acknowledging and affirming your relationship with each other.

- Provide babies with a variety of resources that make sounds. Notice if they choose a particular item to get your attention. Use simple press and response toys and objects they can bang together.

- Introduce books that have sounds, textures and smells. Give the baby undivided attention while you share the book; talking, pointing at the pictures, touching the textures and snuggling close.

- Pick up the early signals that your key babies make when they are hungry or tired. Make notes so that other staff are aware and can respond when you are absent. In this way, the babies can be attended to before they become unduly distressed.

Toddlers

Feeling accepted by key adults and peers confirms to young children that they are valued and underpins their feeling of self-worth. Through the positive responses they receive from others, they develop the conviction and the reassurance that they are lovable. However, if the responses are negative, their self-belief is challenged. Children have many diverse strategies for getting noticed, trying to say 'I am here. Look at me, I am an OK person'. Some children employ negative behaviour to achieve this; they are disobedient, clown around, whine, are clingy or too eager to please. Some may be reluctant and avoid attention, even trying to become invisible – as if saying 'Don't shine the spotlight on me'. These behaviours may indicate underlying insecurities. How key adults respond to this can have significant long-term effects on a child's well-being.

Practical activities

- Circle Time is 'together time' and the activities help young children to feel accepted as part of the group. Younger children may need prompting and the adult can start by saying 'I am glad you are here today so I am going to give everybody a smile', ending with a smile for the circle. The children repeat the opening of the sentence 'I am glad to be here today. I am going to . . .' Alternatively, start with 'It's good to be me because . . .' If a child can't think or doesn't want to say anything, he says 'Pass'. He can always join in when ready.

- Give permission to speak at Circle Time by passing round a special object, for example a lovely shell. Establish the ground rules: if you hold the shell, it is your turn and everybody listens. This helps a child who is shy and curbs those who are over-enthusiastic.

- Facilitate the forming and strengthening of peer friendships – allow the children to choose where and with whom they sit, eat and play. Acknowledge those who have become Friendship Buddies. Early friendships are often quite brief, sometimes traumatic, and may be based around current interests or a shared schema.

- Create opportunities and provide resources where children can try out and develop their own dreams: being a pop star, an athlete or a super hero. Celebrate their achievements: 'Tom is good at . . . ', 'Tina makes great . . . '

- Ensure that each child's special treasures are respected and kept safely. Provide their own space/peg/box or drawer with their name, photograph or favourite picture on it. Acknowledge their particular likes and dislikes: 'Ali, is this your favourite Teddy?'

- Make sure that staff use the children's names frequently during the day. In this way, the children know they are being recognised, noticed, accepted and acknowledged.

- Story telling provides a starting point for talking with the children and gives them a chance to express their feelings. Ask what they think, what they feel, what they would have done.

Outcomes for the child

- Receiving attention means being acknowledged (not getting attention can lead to a feeling of low self-esteem).
- Knowing that you can communicate and are listened to.
- Feeling special and that you are seen as an individual.

Focus points

After nine months in the womb babies instinctively know what they need to grow and develop. During their early months, they rely totally on their parents and carers and require a great deal of one-to-one attention just to meet their physical needs (food, rest, personal comfort) and also their emotional needs. In an early childcare setting babies and young children may feel the need to assert their personalities in order to get noticed. Children learn through their experiences and some discover that by adopting certain inappropriate behaviours they get adults' laughter and attention (it worked for them in the past). They may overplay this behaviour, glorying in the attention given by adults but not realising when it's time to stop or that their behaviour has now become unwelcome. They get confused when what was funny five minutes ago has now worn thin and they are being ignored, or worse, reprimanded. Babies and young children look to adults for signals of correct/incorrect behaviour.

Staff discussion

- How do staff decide who to give their attention to and when? Is time given equally or are some children more demanding than others? Discuss this and consider how you deal with those children who always or rarely seek attention.
- Discuss with parents/carers how their children get attention at home. What strategies do they use? Are these the same as those used in day care?
- How do staff discover a child's qualities, interests and skills; what they are, what they can do well, how others respond to them? What action do staff take to support them?
- Are staff able to give unconditional acceptance, without bias or being judgemental, accepting children 'warts and all'?

2. Enjoyment

Note whether babies are able to feel physically close and enjoy being with you.

(*Birth to Three Matters*)

Babies

Babies want to be comforted and nurtured and are able to form intense emotional attachments, not only with their parents/carers but also with others. They begin to experience new opportunities to develop deep, trusting and secure relationships when they attend day care. A small number of babies may have insecure emotions and do not respond to their key person. Likewise, the key person may not bond naturally with every baby in her care. Placing their baby in day care can cause conflicting emotions for parents/carers such as a feeling of jealousy at the closeness of their baby with the key person or even inadequacies about their parenting skills and lack of self-esteem. When babies feel distressed it is vitally important that they have a special person to turn to for comfort. When the key worker quickly recognises and responds to the babies' signals, the period of distress is minimised.

Practical activities

- Plan quiet times when the baby is held and talked to softly. Look outside at the flowers and birds and listen to the wind chimes. Create dancing lights by tilting a mirror at the sun to create light patterns.

- Cradle baby in your arms and sing softly or say rhymes. Hold her securely on your knee and bounce gently, singing 'Horsey, horsey'. Look for opportunities to develop close physical contact when playing.

- Use teddies and soft toys for baby to cuddle and kiss, demonstrating loving behaviour. Talk to toys with the babies and use them to encourage closeness.

Toddlers

Young children and toddlers reach a stage when they assert their independence, explore and stretch boundaries yet they still need to know that they can return to their carer to enjoy cuddles and closeness. With the development of self-confidence and competence, relationships with practitioners and peers becomes more relaxed; the children begin to understand humour, enjoy a joke, show joy and happiness. At the same time they are developing empathy – an awareness that others have feelings too – and show this in thoughtful acts of kindness and care. It is important that children understand that having fun and making jokes should never involve teasing, ridiculing or hurting someone else.

Practical activities

Although having fun and being happy is an attitude of mind, not an activity, some planned activities may help to increase these positive emotions.

- Create a laughter tape. Hearing people laugh triggers the impulse to laugh.
- Make a soft and sparkly tickling stick. The anticipation of a tickle can produce lots of giggles yet if done unexpectedly, if the child is unaware, it may create displeasure and fear. Tickle the feet or the neck lightly with the stick. Tickling requires trust and helps with bonding. It should not be used to tease.
- Provide full-length crazy mirrors where children can see their reflections distorted. These can be made by bending acrylic mirrors forward or backwards.
- Have special moments when children can choose to sit quietly, listen to music and stories, look at books, cuddle a softy toy.
- Play a game to get someone to laugh. One child stands in the centre of the circle while the others ask questions. The child in the centre can only answer with the word 'sausages'. When someone in the circle is caught laughing, he/she swaps with the child at the centre.
- Have physical fun where the children are in control – running, jumping, standing still, being pushed on a swing.
- Provide opportunities for children to be responsible and care for animals. If live ones are not available, create small world toy play.
- Create opportunities during role play where children take on a caring role.
- Have a large soft toy for children to wrap their arms around and hug.

Outcomes for the child

- Children feel more relaxed with themselves and others.
- Continuing development of trust.
- Social and emotional development.

Focus points

Laughter is said to be the best medicine as it has physiological, psychological and spiritual benefits. It relaxes the mind and body and creates a bond, a connection between people. Being able to have fun, feeling happy, is an attitude of mind, a disposition. It is hard to define or measure yet the outcome has many benefits and a relaxed, happy person is likely to make friends more easily. It is recognised that babies and young children thrive on the feeling that they are accepted and enjoy the comfort of being held. Carers respond to children in different ways and being physically close with babies and young children may present staff with concerns about child protection. Talking as a staff team and sharing views about what is appropriate behaviour in terms of physical contact can help to alleviate these concerns.

Staff discussion

- Ensure that all staff have appropriate training and understand the polices and guidelines related to child protection.
- Staff must be impartial and give physical closeness evenly to babies and young children. If other staff notice any favouritism or exclusion, there needs to be a system where the situation can be monitored. Above all staff should be professional and provide quality provision.
- Some cultures are less physical when displaying emotions or affections. This needs to be taken into account by key staff. Look to develop training in the knowledge and awareness of cultural mores.
- Plan times for staff to relax and have fun together.

3. Relationships

Plan specific opportunities for all the children in your care to build secure relationships with you.

(*Birth to Three Matters*)

Babies

Being able to demonstrate a warm and open feeling towards babies makes them feel good. Your face gives clear signals that show your true feelings and babies are skilled at picking up subtle signs and are quick to respond if there is tension or if you are preoccupied. They need to feel safe and comfortable when held. It is important that the practitioner is relaxed and sitting correctly in order to hold the baby securely. Practitioners can develop upper body pain and back pain if they do not have the right seating.

Practical activities

- Create an area/zone where both adult and baby are comfortable, using nursing chairs, soft cushions and toys.
- Collect photographs that highlight facial expressions. Ideally, these should be natural and show real feelings, such as happiness, surprise, wonder or tears (see Resources). Laminate them and talk about them with the baby or use them to make a display.
- Be aware that even young babies are sensitive and can sense if adults are laughing about them or talking about them over their head. Talking about a baby in a negative way is destructive and unhelpful when trying to form secure relationships.

Toddlers

Developing shared feelings helps to create a strong bond and this can be achieved by being sincere, relaxed, laughing and having fun with children and showing appropriate tenderness. As a young child/toddler experiments with emerging independence, he will feel confident to move further away from his carer yet still needs to know he can return when he needs reassurance, to ask a question or just to be physically close. Toddlers still enjoy snuggles and cuddles. They are only able to judge their own worth and competence by the reactions of others (adults and peer group) – how they are seen by them, respected by them. With the development of language, they can ask for help and express their feelings.

During this period a young child will show signs that he is developing empathy, and is able to care about other's feelings.

Practical activities

- Once a week choose a child to be King/Queen for the day. Have a specially decorated chair or throne, a big badge to declare it's 'Sally's special day' so that everyone in the setting is aware and acknowledges that this carries privileges, the freedom to choose what to do, who to play with, which toys to play with, be first to make a selection. At Circle Time, ask the group and other staff for special comments about 'Sally'. During the day take digital photographs/video, record comments and create a record of the day to take home and share with parents/carers. Choose a fair method for selecting the special child, for example names hidden under flaps (like an Advent calendar), names inside straws. Ensure the group is not too large so that children don't have to wait too long for their day.

- During the year, look for opportunities for the children to have contact with and observe baby animals, lambs, rabbits, kittens or ducklings. This should trigger feelings of tenderness, protection and care. Discuss how they had to be looked after when they were first born. Collect photos of babies and young animals.

- Show video stories that include animals, such as Bambi, and talk about how the feelings of happiness and sadness that the images generate.

- Observe those children who show care and concern to others such as trying to comfort another when distressed: 'Let me kiss it better'. Provide caring activities such as Mummy, Daddy and baby play, hospital play, or set up a vet's surgery for the toy animals.

Outcomes for the child

- Learning that it is OK to demonstrate feelings.
- Learning that others have feelings too.
- Developing trust and bonding with others.

Focus points

The setting reflects how the staff respect the babies and children. If it is tatty or cluttered with mismatched resources, it implies that this is what the children are worth. The environment should be calm with interesting objects attractively presented, inviting and touching the senses. If beautiful items are out of sight or out of reach, the children will never have the chance to handle them or appreciate them. How can they begin to understand and appreciate what delicate or fragile means if they have never been given the chance or the confidence to hold something special?

If we want young children to become competent yet always choose what they play with, or provide templates, they won't believe in their own capabilities; they will think they are not capable or that their choices are not respected.

Staff discussion

- Observe how babies and young children's facial expressions and body language show what they are feeling.

- Encourage staff discussion about their life experiences, values and core beliefs. These may have a direct influence on how they react and respond to babies and young children.

4. Boundaries

Encourage all children to participate in making any rules and help them to understand expectations and boundaries.

(Birth to Three Matters)

Babies

Babies begin to realise that there are life rules. A young baby starting to crawl or do something that is dangerous looks to an adult to see if she should continue. A firm 'No' and serious eye contact confirms the rule. In a similar way when a baby is given a biscuit and the practitioner says 'ta' they begin to gain the beginnings of good manners. Eventually, after reinforcements, the baby understands that saying thank you (ta) comes after receiving something. In order to work, expectations and boundaries need to be consistently applied by the whole team.

Practical activities

- Play a game where you pass items to and fro to a baby and say 'ta' or 'thank you' (or use their own language) each time you receive it, smile and make eye contact.

- Banging a spoon on a bowl. Show the baby how to be gentle and to make contact with the bowl, not another baby. Hold her hand and demonstrate using a soft voice. Reinforce with smiles and a nod each time she gets it right.

- Once a baby is learning to crawl, provide a long runner for her and encourage her to reach you at the other end. Hold out your arms, smile and praise her when she reaches you.

- Use distractions to stop unwanted behaviour. Collect items that make an interesting noise such as shaking coins in a plastic bottle; attract attention through sudden movement or favourite cuddly toys. Praise when they stop the unwanted behaviour.

Toddlers

Children feel secure when they have known boundaries but once they become two or three years old they will test them to see just how far they can go, pushing them and the adults to the limit. Rules and boundaries have to be consistently applied, seen to be fair, be few in number and be realistic for the children to meet. Young children will question 'Why?' and the reasons should be discussed and, if possible, agreed together. Most boundaries and rules are there for reasons of safety, hygiene or protection.

Practical activities

- Certain rules will be set in stone, for example not leaving the premises without a known adult. Others are for the well-being of the children and help to create a harmonious atmosphere. Encourage the children to talk about and agree a simple rule such as use of the outdoor play equipment and wheelie toys. Once agreed, display the rule with a simple cartoon-type figure or symbol and refer to it before they go outside.

- Once a rule/limit has been understood reinforce with clear signals or non-verbal gestures to remind the children or to reinforce the rule: direct eye contact and a shake of the head, or if noise is an issue, pretend to zip up the lip or place a finger on the lip and say 'shush'. Have a paper plate with a smiley face on one side and a sad one the other.

- Use signals such as a bell, a shaker or a tune to alert the children that it's time to stop and tidy up or to gather for Circle Time.

- Ask the children how they feel when another child refuses to share, snatches their toy or screams and bites. Introduce a story or a hand puppet to start a discussion (see Resources). Make it fun – exaggerate the point so it is humorous but has a real message. Talk about the consequences of actions and other people's feelings. Introduce the old saying 'Do as you would be done by'.

- Have clear and consistent outcomes about what happens if the rule/limit is deliberately broken. This will depend on the seriousness of the situation. It may simply be distracting the child with a toy or an activity, finding another play mate or having 'time out'. It is important to stress that the behaviour, not the child, is unwanted. If they want to say 'sorry', it has to be genuine. If implementing 'time out', let the child decide when he feels he is ready to return.

Outcomes for the child

- Boundaries help to provide a feeling of security.
- Simple rules help babies and young children learn positive behaviour patterns.
- Children learn to be responsible for their own actions.

Focus points

A baby employs all her senses decoding, watching and listening, learning to understand and pick up clues from the adult world. Babies and young children look to adults for guidance as to what is desirable/undesirable behaviour. When adults are unresponsive or inconsistent in their reactions to a child's behaviour, he has no clear guidelines. When reactions are negative, he concludes that *he* is unlovable or at fault rather than his behaviour.

Boundaries are invisible and intangible and need to be made clear and understood. Some limits define the boundary to ensure that behaviour is unacceptable if it hurts or upsets someone else. A balance needs to be maintained between keeping the children safe yet helping them develop independence and personal responsibility while encouraging exploration and the development of new skills.

Staff discussion

- The personal boundaries that surround us are based on our own values and beliefs and are what define us as individuals. Spend time as a team discussing the principles, values and beliefs about boundaries that you all agree are of the utmost importance when working with babies and young children.

- How can you tell if a baby is deliberately ignoring boundaries, pushing limits or simply has not yet understood what is acceptable?
- What strategies and support do staff employ that help babies and young children to learn how to recognise and control their negative feelings?
- How often do staff actively praise good behaviour with specific and constructive comments such as 'You were very well behaved at the snack table Leon; you said please and thank you'.
- Do you communicate the rules used in the setting to parents/carers so that they are aware of and understand them?

5. Expectations

Children need to feel others are positive towards them, and to experience realistic expectations in order to become competent, assertive and self-assured.

(*Birth to Three Matters*)

Babies

Babies have emotional feelings and need to feel that others acknowledge them and feel positive towards them. This makes them feel good and improves their well-being. Babies can sense when there is not a positive reaction from their carer and this can cause them to feel detached, insecure, even vulnerable. Give physical signals such as a welcome smile, warmth and open body language.

There is an expectation for babies to match their developmental stage yet each one will achieve in her own time according to her own unique personality. When babies meet or excel in any activities, they feel competent and are more able to become assertive and self-assured.

Practical activities

● Hold the baby and look into a mirror together as you sing happy songs. Note the baby's reactions as you laugh and smile.

● Collect fun items such as laughing boxes, smiley toys and tickly feathers.

● Choose activities that allow a close partnership with the baby, for example lavender dough – squeezing, touching, pulling, rolling it together. It is tactile and relaxes both baby and practitioner.

Toddlers

Young children and toddlers develop at their own rate, often in fits and starts, so that within any group there will be a wide difference of abilities, skills and understanding. It is said that children will reach up to or down to the expectations that you place on them. Expecting too little can be as just as detrimental as expecting too much. Certain expectations, such as respecting the rights and feelings of others, need to be clearly stated to the children just as their own rights need to be clearly established that carers will respond to them, care for them and keep them safe.

Practical activities

● When choosing games and equipment seek resources that are appropriate for the skills and interests of the group: too demanding and the child may fail; too simple and the resource won't be challenging enough.

● Use positive language, for example 'Walk inside' instead of 'Don't run'. 'The blocks are for building not throwing. Let's see how high we can make this building' instead of 'Don't throw the blocks'.

● Expect the children to be responsible. For example, develop systems for them to sign in on arrival. Create Velcro name labels that they attach to a board or name cards to transfer to a Welcome box. Later the carer checks the names and gives a positive comment such as 'Here is Matt's card. Hello Matt, good to see you'.

● Organise a café-style snack area where the children decide when they are hungry and what they want to eat or drink. Have a selection of healthy snacks/drinks to choose from.

- Organise activities so that the children can indicate what they want to play with, where and with whom. Discuss options at Circle Time and provide simple methods of selection, for example a magnetic self-portrait (photograph) to fix onto an activity board. To allow for popular activities agree on a time slot and provide a timer that rings to signal 'Change now'.

- Expect that each child will tidy up after free play. Make this easy by having clearly labelled containers and child accessible storage.

Outcomes for the child

- Feeling valued.
- Growth of self-esteem.
- The development of competence and self-assurance.

Focus points

It is essential that practitioners have a good understanding of the stages of development in early childhood and yet accept that each child has had his own unique experiences that shape and define him as an individual. Babies and young children are ready to explore and learn but they are beginners with few previous experiences to draw upon. It is a fragile time when the negative feelings of failure, making mistakes, not getting it right or being rejected by the group are hard to take and can cause damage to self-esteem and confidence and eventually their learning potential. Practitioners need to concentrate on what each child can do and build upon it by providing a broad range of experiences celebrating each small success.

Parent/carers' expectations for their child may not be the same as those of the practitioner. Some cultures have high expectations for the development of young people's learning while others view early childhood as a period of play and discovery. The early years from birth to three are for making exciting discoveries about self, people and the world – not for trying to act like a four- or five-year-old.

Staff discussion

- Sometimes we are unaware of how we are perceived by others. For example, a practitioner may feel nervous about meeting parents/carers and as a result talks too quickly, too loudly, laughs or becomes dictatorial. Discuss with staff what they feel are their own strengths and weaknesses.

- Video tape a session of practitioners and babies/young children together. Discuss how the staff use their body language, gestures, facial expressions and language to give positive feedback to babies and young children. What messages do they convey to the children?

- Explore the techniques for observation and assessment of staff as used in the Effective Early Learning training programme (EEL) (see Resources for Chapter 2).

- Does the printed communication given to parents explain clearly the philosophy and ethos of the setting?

6. Emotional boundaries

> Young children strive for responses from others, which confirm, contribute to, or challenge their understanding of themselves.
>
> (*Birth to Three Matters*)

Babies

All babies are different and some may appear to seek attention which causes a disruption. Practitioners have to use their professional knowledge, understanding and skills to assess the reasons behind this behaviour and find ways to deal with it. Very tearful babies demand attention, one-to-one time and energy. Dealing with extreme emotions or behaviour can be upsetting for all involved and can mean that routines are thrown into disarray and plans are abandoned. Ensuring that babies' physical needs are met effectively can help to eliminate some of the possible causes of attention seeking.

Practical activities

- Keep a collection of distracters: soft toys, some which make a noise, puppets, etc. that are only used when babies need attention.

- Track a baby for a session and note the times when attention seeking is most obvious. Is there a pattern? It may mean reviewing the way the session or the adult's time is organised.

- Consider your vocabulary and replace negatives such as 'Don't' and 'Stop' with positive instructions such as 'Lets do...' Encourage all staff to watch and listen and use this approach.

Toddlers

Your freedom to swing your arms ends where my nose begins.
(from Alison Miller's *Living in Families Effectively*, www.lifeseminars.com/askalison)

It is the feelings we have deep inside that make us react to people and situations the way we do. Young children and toddlers are still trying to recognise and learn to control these often disturbing feelings. As they mature, they will learn that we all have these feelings but we can choose which ones come out. This means that during a session there may suddenly be challenging and upsetting outbursts, tears and confusion. These young children will still seek comfort, understanding and special toys to regain their composure. Some children lack the language skills to describe their feelings and in frustration get physical and lash out. It is important that adults take account of the need for safety of themselves, the child and others.

Practical activities

- Introduce games that require the players to wait their turn or to share resources. For example, play matching games like 'Snap' or 'Bingo'. Start with a pair of children then increase to a small group of three or four.

- Provide words that identify emotions: happy, sad and angry. Ask the children how they know when they are excited or afraid. What do they feel like when waiting to go to a party or opening a parcel, or if they have to visit somewhere new? Make interesting boxes – one colourfully decorated and tied with a ribbon, the other wrapped in old paper, a funny shape. Which one do they want to open? Be sure there is a nice surprise waiting in both of them. Decide on words to describe good feelings, for example 'soft' and 'furry' or bad ones like 'hard' and 'spikey'.

- Agree on an area or a special place where children can go when they are feeling upset. It may be when they feel too angry or just needing to be quiet. Have comfort toys, books and cushions available.

Outcomes for the child

- Attention seeking becomes moderated.
- Babies and children become more self-controlled.

Focus points

Practitioners need to address a child's strong emotions; they are very real to the child. Talk quietly, soothingly and without criticism while you try to discover what is upsetting them. Once they have calmed down ask what they could have done, instead of kicking or biting etc. Put the emphasis on the behaviour. The younger the child, the more influential is the adult's role in helping him understand his emotions and mould his behaviour. If a child is constantly seeking negative attention, try to discover if there is a deeper issue bubbling away below the surface. Consider the process of finding this out and at what point would parents/carers be consulted.

Staff discussion

- Consider the well-being of the staff. How are they supported if they reach 'the end of the line' and find dealing with certain children too demanding or too challenging?
- Some staff may feel that it is best to ignore a demanding child. Does being ignored make a child feel acknowledged and affirmed? Discuss if the staff deal with attention seeking in a proactive or reactive way?
- Would discussing negative emotions and behaviour with parents compromise or confirm the PR (public relations) message that the setting is a happy, caring and responsive environment?

References

British Association for Early Childhood Education (2000) *Living, Loving and Learning*. London: Early Education (contact office@early-education.org.uk for photographic exhibition with explanatory text).

DfES (Department for Education and Skills) (2002) *Birth to Three Matters: A Framework to Support Children in their Earliest Years*. London: DfES.

DfES (Department for Education and Skills) (2003) *Every Child Matters*. London: DfES.

DfES (Department for Education and Skills)/DWP (Department for Work and Pensions) (2003) *National Standards for Under 8s Day Care and Childminding (Full Day Care)*. London: DfES.

Edwards, D. (2002) *My Naughty Little Sister* series. London: Egmont Books.

Rogers, C. (1969) *Freedom to Learn: Studies of the Person*. Columbus, OH: Charles Merrill.

Sure Start (2005) *Personal, Social and Emotional Development* – Training materials. London: DfES.

Resources

Life Seminars – a unique parenting programme providing advice on *Living in Families Effectively* by Dr Alison Miller – see www.lifeseminars.com/askalison

PC Software from Sherston 'The Not So Naughty Stories', aimed at 3–6 years, interactive whiteboards; could be useful for initiating a discussion – visit www.sherston.com

Centre for Research in Early Childhood, St Thomas Centre, Bell Barn Road, Attwood Green, Birmingham B15 2AF

PEEP (Peers Early Education Partnership), PEEP Learning Ltd – see www.peep.org.uk

4 Developing self-assurance

Introduction

Each baby and young child arrives at a setting as a unique individual with many traits and aspects of their personality already formed. Some arrive with a bright, open smile and others are tearful and shy. One may open the door with confidence, ready and willing to take on any new experience, while another appears bored and disinterested. Although children are born with a range of emotions, their self-concept is formed and reinforced by the reactions of others. They imitate adults, copying their gestures, tone of voice, phrases, and also pick up subtle signals about belief systems, values and judgements. If adults wish to promote qualities such as sharing, caring and friendship, they need to demonstrate this in their own relationships with each other and with the children. Some babies and young children may have been hurt, rejected or abused and, as a defence against future painful feelings, build a wall around themselves which affects their whole personality. A child's view of himself can in turn influence how others see him and so becomes a self-fulfilling prophesy: he feels insignificant and so is seen as insignificant by others. It is important that adults and key carers emphasise positive concepts and self-belief and create opportunities for them to flourish.

Childcarers have a difficult task of uncovering each child's potential and capabilities by understanding and assessing the signals they project. Brief but careful observations, such as time sampling, done on a regular basis can help to provide clues to personality and identify what is 'of the moment' and minor, and what are significant patterns of behaviour.

A childcare setting is like a small community where everyone is connected with a common goal. Babies and young children can be viewed as passive receivers or as active participants who are valued for their contribution. The ethos and organisation may be adult led, child initiated or a mixture of the two, but the aim is to help each child to develop into a well-adjusted, self-confident person who is willing to tackle new experiences and be able to form close and secure relationships.

1. Self-reliance

Note how babies become confident in exploring what they can do with less dependence on adults.

(Birth to Three Matters)

Babies

Observing babies tells us about their personalities, moods, needs and how they are developing. Physical needs – food, sleep and being clean – are a high priority and take up much of the practitioner's time. It is important that babies have periods of socialisation/play with each other and with their key carer but also short times when they can explore, make choices and play by themselves. The secret is to plan for this so the key person can quietly observe them. Ideally, having a digital camera on hand, with a timer function, can provide useful evidence to support these observations. It is essential that these periods are not too long in case the baby gets upset or anxious. Of course, there is an absolute necessity to adhere to all the National Day Care Standards at all times.

Practical activities

- Set up a short 'Tummy time' session where the baby can choose what to play with from a limited selection. Think carefully about the items you provide and what you wish to observe – for example, physical development and the fine control of hands and fingers might include a collection of rattles, soft toys and silk scarves.

- Babies have varying rest patterns so in the baby room some will wake up while others are still sleeping. Ensure there is a calm atmosphere when a baby wakes, with a familiar carer close by to say 'Hello' and give a cuddle. Play quiet music and have 'over the cot' mobiles to look at. Create a 'waking up bag' with interesting contents to explore and soft toys to play with. Allow the baby a short period alone to wake up.

- Create a small, calm enclosed area where the baby can play alone. Fix netting (such as bed mosquito nets) and if possible, have soft coloured lights that shine through the net, cushions to support the baby and a basket of natural objects to explore.

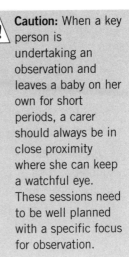

Caution: When a key person is undertaking an observation and leaves a baby on her own for short periods, a carer should always be in close proximity where she can keep a watchful eye. These sessions need to be well planned with a specific focus for observation.

Toddlers

Toddlers have varying levels of concentration and these depend on their physical and mental development that interacts with their feelings. They have bursts of energy and need to be allowed to move and be mobile; hence, the floor play area needs to be larger than table top areas. Concentration is likely to be sustained if there are adequate resources – for example, double the quantity of construction toys to enable children to access and sustain their play. The provision of activities that meet the children's interests and needs will promote motivation and can be recognised by clear involvement signals.

Practical activities

- Plan to have outside play times quite early, when energy levels are high: around 10:00 a.m. is better than waiting until 11:00 a.m. Find out the times that toddlers have had breakfast, and if they actually ate anything. Depending on the information received, think carefully about how and when snacks are offered.

- Put construction toys onto acrylic mirror tiles so that youngsters can view their constructions from different angles. This can encourage sustainability and concentration.

- Provide aquarium nets to scoop up items in the water tray. Provide spaghetti tongs to get objects from below the surface. This will encourage hand–eye co-ordination along with concentration.

- In the sand tray, supply colanders, sink strainers, tea strainers and sieves that allow the free flow of sand. Having a variety will sustain the children's interest.

- Help children to feel they are part of the group by encouraging them to be responsible for watering the plants, feeding fish, tidying up the dolls' clothes, returning resources. Have a child-sized brush and dustpan for spills.

- Make the waste bin into a 'Hungry Monster' and encourage the children to 'feed' it at tidy up time.

- Organise simple cooking activities (under supervision) such as buttering bread and making sandwiches, biscuits, cakes and jellies (sugar free). Use them for the group as snack time choices.

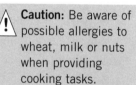

Caution: Be aware of possible allergies to wheat, milk or nuts when providing cooking tasks.

Outcomes for the child

- Developing self-assurance and self-confidence.
- Increased awareness of own strengths.
- Beginning to value own abilities.

Focus points

During toddlerhood children develop very definite ideas about what they want to do, and will often try to stretch limits or test an adult's reactions to their behaviour. They learn that they can ask for what they want but it is also a time when they learn that they can say 'No' and discover there can be unpleasant consequences to their decisions. Refusing to take part in an activity, being stubborn or selfish and unkind can provoke a negative response. Offer clear alternatives such as 'Would you like to do this, or that?' or 'Let's do this and then we can do that'. This gives the child the choice and ability to make a decision without too many confusing options.

Staff discussion

- As a team discuss how, when and why observations are made. How are observations used to inform future practice?
- Consider the type of resources needed to ensure that the flow of play is not disrupted.
- Remember that every day offers the possibility of a fresh start.
- How do staff respond to a child that is demanding or unattractive? Look for ways to support that child and to discover what is best for him.

2. Self-assurance

To develop independence babies need to feel safe and secure within healthy relationships with key people.

(*Birth to Three Matters*)

Babies

Self-assurance is a firm belief in one's own powers and leads to confidence and independence. Providing a safe environment where this can happen is inevitably linked to the quality of the provision and the skills of practitioners. They make the decisions of where, when, how and with what a baby plays. Babies are by nature inquisitive, and giving them real opportunities to explore and discover for themselves builds their confidence and their ability to become independent. Just 'occupying' babies will not do this and ultimately their self-assurance will not flourish. Babies move from helplessness to self-assurance, from flailing involuntary movements to purposeful and precise motor skills and from quiet contemplation to bubbling personalities.

Practical activities

- Plan time for daily physical exercises with key persons. These only have to be short five-minute sessions. Use music and toys so that babies get used to using both right- and left-hand sides of their body, for example passing a soft ball from hand to hand or rolling the ball to each other. This time will also reinforce closeness and bonding with each other.

- Plan time for daily exploration. Place familiar and new items on a textured mat. These can range from household objects to natural materials or nursery toys. Observe which ones the babies choose to explore.

- Make time during the day for close physical contact with the baby, giving a hug, a smile and soft words. Even the most independent child needs physical reassurance.

Toddlers

A toddler grows little by little, gradually mastering life skills, so he will need understanding and patience as with any long-term process. The key person can only be a guide. The physical development of a young child's body is not necessarily in sync with his intellectual development and added to this are the emotional and social aspects. During these early years toddlers and young children go through a helter-skelter of emotions: at times they appear strong and powerful and then regress to baby-like behaviour, seeking comforters and reassurance. They may be able to walk and run yet want to ride in a pushchair. They are eager to learn and master a whole range of new skills that will give freedom, independence and opportunities for socialisation.

Practical activities

- Provide toys such as fastening dolls that help children develop manipulative skills associated with dressing: large buttons and button holes, zips, Velcro, laces and toggles that they can practise on. Chubby hands are slow and unco-ordinated. Hand–eye co-ordination is needed to match a button to the button hole.

- Toddlers can usually get undressed but have trouble with sleeves and fastenings when trying to get dressed. When putting on a T-shirt they have to work out that the large hole is for the head and the smaller ones are for the arms. If they are getting upset and struggling, intervene with a compliment: 'You have tried really hard; sometimes it is good to rest – let me help you'.

- Playing with dough and other manipulative materials will help to strengthen the hands, fingers and thumbs.

- Provide bowls and cutlery in the home play area. Use dried pulses for the children to practise feeding their dolls. Have a selection of clothes to dress dolls and teddies. Include some that are too big or too small. Observe how the children select and fit them correctly.

- Trying to distinguish small differences, such as which is the left or right shoe, is difficult. Decorate the shoes with stickers so that they can tell them apart. Provide games and puzzles that encourage the children to look closely for differences.

- Most toddlers will be toilet trained but there may be 'accidents'. Deal with these calmly and quickly so as not to embarrass the child or make him feel he has failed.

> ⚠ **Caution:** Check with parents/carers before sticking anything onto the children's shoes.

- Toddlers are often unco-ordinated and take tumbles. Staff need to reassure them without negating their feelings, for example saying 'Ouch that must have really hurt, Josh. Let me hold you for a while' rather than dismissing with 'You are OK'.

Outcomes for the child

- Development of self-assurance, both physical and mental abilities.
- Becoming an independent thinker.
- A healthy interdependence with practitioner.

Focus points

Early childhood is a critical time in a child's life and the impact of good or bad experiences has long-reaching effects. The qualities that the key person brings are vital in the development of babies and young children. It is an area where the most experienced, sensitive, intuitive and skilled carers are needed and should be valued. Using corrective language acknowledges a child's difficulties while dealing with his emotional state. For example, 'Ahmed, I know it is hard to wait your turn, but when John has finished it is your turn on the bike' or 'Ow! That hurts me when you hit my arm to get attention. I know you are excited but you must not hit me'.

Staff discussion

- Encourage staff to research the area of self-assurance and share the information at a staff meeting. Look in college books, articles in professional magazines, on the internet. Discuss ways to improve this very important area of care.

- Ask each member of staff to select one child for observation on self-assurance, compare, contrast and discuss the behaviour, dispositions and attitudes that indicate levels of self-assurance.

- Explain to parents/carers why it is helpful to dress their children in clothes that are simple to put on and the satisfaction the children have when they can do it for themselves.

- 'You can't run before you can walk' – what are the stages a child needs to have mastered before he can run? What opportunities and encouragement are needed?

- Take a look at simple tasks such as dressing or feeding and break down the skills needed into small achievable steps.

- Are there simple ways that children can help around the setting to give them a sense of responsibility?

3. Valuing abilities

Note how children express their own confidence and sense of self-assurance, by showing they value what they and others do.

(*Birth to Three Matters*)

Babies

Confidence is an indicator of each person's belief about him/herself and links closely to his/her self-esteem and self-assurance. The belief that we are lovable and cared for is the most basic emotional need. The reaction of others gives us an indication of our self-worth, telling us that we are significant, that our opinions matter and others value us. These deep core beliefs are developed in early childhood and affect the way we see ourselves as valuable individuals.

Practical activities

- Confidence comes from positive feedback. When a baby has done something well, feed this back to parents. Ask them to repeat a similar activity at home. It can be something as simple as clapping or slapping the baby's high chair tray as you sing a song with her. In this way, the baby's actions are reinforced with twice the praise.

- Watch babies' faces when they have achieved something. Capture these moments on camera but don't forget to celebrate with a cuddle, a clap and a 'Well done!'

- Developing physical skills is an important area for a baby which is linked to self-confidence. Examples include being able to self-feed, pulling up on a bar or crawling to reach objects.

- Log carefully and record babies' development so that other key persons know what they are and what they are capable of.

Toddlers

Having self-confidence is the belief that you can achieve and that you can be yourself. It provides an internal resilience that allows a person to persist in an activity and overcome difficulties or obstacles. If a young child encounters a problem, such as spilling juice when trying to pour from a jug, it is important that he does not feel it is his fault. Look to see if the jug is too heavy, the cup is too small, the height and angle of the table are wrong. Without fuss, encourage him to get a cloth and clean it up and then make the necessary adjustments so he can do it. A child who is secure and confident is better able to manage his own behaviour and is able to make and sustain friendships and relationships. If he believes that he is clumsy, stupid or naughty, it may become a self-fulfilling prophecy and he will not try as he expects to fail.

Practical activities

- Introduce an induction programme for new admissions. Encourage parents/carers and children to visit the setting together for short periods prior to starting. This can help to allay the fears and anxieties of both the parents/carers and their children, easing the transition from home to the setting. They will get to know the layout of the environment, where the toilets are, what happens at mealtimes and meet key carers. It is important that children can separate from their parents without undue stress and may even look forward to the new experiences that await them.

- Outside play can challenge even the most self-assured and confident child. Provide regular sessions outside which support the development of both large and small motor skills. Examples might include roundabouts and parking bays for bikes to negotiate, water trays with a variety of jugs, large and small, to develop pouring skills.

- When encouraging children to contribute during Circle Time use open questioning techniques. These allow each child to express opinions or offer suggestions without the fear of giving a wrong answer. Closed questions only require a 'Yes or No' answer; therefore some children may be reluctant to commit and 'be wrong'. Encourage all the children to contribute by singing, saying a rhyme and clapping to celebrate even the smallest effort. Take photographs of these times and use them to talk with each toddler and tell him how well he is doing. Print the words of songs and rhymes and encourage the children to take them home to share with family.

- Ask the children, 'If you could make a wish, what would it be?' This can give an insight into what they feel is important to be or to have.

- Break down the steps required to master a skill, for example using scissors. Prior to using scissors the children need to have had practice developing manipulative skills, for example putting pegs on a washing line, around the edges of a cardboard box or pegs into holes. Have round-ended scissors that cut well, not blunt or plastic. Thin card is easier to cut than paper; fabric is more difficult still. Draw a thick black line to practise cutting and have large pictures to cut around. Create an 'I can' book with digital photos and text that show each step. This can cement the feeling of achievement.

- Feeding and potty training are important aspects of toddlerhood. To develop these children must build up their confidence and self-assurance. Use role play with teddies and dollies so that the toddlers can act out and tell the toys how well they are doing

Outcomes for the child

- Development of independence.
- Growing in confidence.
- Developing as an individual.
- Being proud of achievements.

Focus points

Babies and young children need physical and mental tasks which they can manipulate and get pleasure from on their own. This does not mean that the practitioner simply puts out resources and retires – far from it. To gauge the levels of confidence that a baby/child has reached we need observations, evaluations and encouragement. A key person trying to promote self-assurance needs to withdraw and observe them from close proximity then intervene at just the right moment. Sometimes babies and young children will fail in developing confidence because the adults have misjudged when to step in and support them, doing so too early or too late. It is said that Thomas Edison made 700 attempts before he created the light bulb. During that time, he learnt why 700 things didn't work. People don't fail; it's just that their plan, their strategies and tactics didn't work this time for this activity.

Staff discussion

- How can we ensure we get the balance right, encouraging confidence yet not letting some children dominate? How do children demonstrate they are confident? Is it by 'blowing their own trumpet' or by what they actually do?
- Encourage staff discussion about their own levels of confidence, perceived strengths and weaknesses. Write down 'I feel confident when . . .' In this way they will begin to have insight and empathise with the babies and young children they work with.
- Discuss the important role they play in the building of the babies' and young children's confidence. What new strategies could they put in place?
- Look for ways of making everyday activities simpler or more challenging to suit the skills of different children, for example table top toys such as puzzles with varying degree of difficulty that require the skill to differentiate.

4. Persistence

Some children may require more time than others to undertake a task. Encouraging them to 'try' and showing you appreciate effort can lead to feelings of self-worth.

(Birth to Three Matters)

Babies

While it is necessary to have knowledge of stages of development, for example when a child is expected to begin to walk or talk, it is important to remember that guidelines are just that – guides. Some babies may be early crawlers but slow talkers, while the reverse is true for others. Meeting diverse needs requires good observational skills, knowledge and the understanding of each individual's progress along his/her own path. Encouraging a baby to try may mean a nod, a smile, a clap and not showing displeasure if she fails. If she doesn't manage the task or quickly becomes disinterested, do not make a big deal. It may mean the baby is not ready or needs to have several demonstrations or even have the activity presented in a different way before she wants to try for herself.

Practical activities

- Examine a task carefully and the skills needed to complete it, for example learning to grasp and hold a spoon. It will depend on the size of the baby's hand, the shape of the handle, the texture and the baby's motivation. Try exploring different materials: are some shapes or textures easier to grip than others? Does introducing food motivate the baby?

- At mealtimes babies respond to food in different ways: some eat slowly, others eat anything, some pick and choose. Practitioners should accept how the children are. However, be aware if a baby's eating habits suddenly change; look for possible reasons.

- Personalise sleep times. Some babies take time to settle down to sleep. At home, they may have special rituals, comforters or sounds so ask parents/carers about this. Attach this information to the cots with Velcro so that all staff are aware and know how to encourage the baby to sleep.

Toddlers

Toddlers need praise when they are really trying to master a skill. A few words will support and sustain them in what they are trying to do. When giving praise focus on a specific action, not on generalisations: for example, 'Mark, you are really good at cutting that paper with the scissors'. If a task is too hard or beyond his capabilities, it will frustrate him; it may even demotivate him from trying another time. When planning an activity for toddlers one has to be fluid: some youngsters will come to it and leave after five minutes, some will stay longer; others will leave and return later. It can help a child to succeed if the skill can be broken down into achievable steps. However, there is no value in reaching a goal that is too 'easy peasy'.

Practical activities

- Collect a range of encouraging phrases to support children's efforts. However, ensure that they aren't used in a false or automatic way that the children will know is empty praise. Show real delight when they discover they can do something for the first time.

- Provide tools to cover the range of emerging skills. For example, when playing with dough, include different sized rollers and cutters to account for the variety of children's manipulative skills.

- Provide a wide range of printing items, such as exotic fruit and vegetables, net curtain squares. Using rollers provides a quick and instant experience and promotes confidence.

- Have mix and match collections of construction toys. Some children will want to accept a challenge while others prefer to have a safe, familiar experience.

- Hide surprises to be uncovered during an activity – for instance, wrap a pretty shell, a single bright feather or a small toy. Share in their delight of the surprise and discovery.

- Teach simple relaxation techniques such as Belly Breathing (see Dennison, 1994). This helps to calm children, quietens their mind and helps them to refocus (this works for practitioners too!).

Outcomes for the child

- Understanding that it's OK to take time, not to hurry to complete a task.
- Individuality is respected.
- Children feel reassured.

Focus points

Not all children want to join in and play with others; some two-year-olds are content to sit and watch. However, by three years of age most have become eager to join a group and enjoy socialisation. A child should never be forced to join in or to attempt something he doesn't feel happy and comfortable with. Key staff can help by using a range of strategies and encouragement but need to be aware of the difference between sensitive and intrusive intervention.

Staff discussion

- Consider how and where a child gets the idea 'I can't do it'. What strategies can you use to encourage a child to try something new? If you know a child's strengths and interests, you can plan for activities that will motivate him to succeed.
- Think about what motivates you: is it the pain or fear of failure, or is it the thought of the pleasure of achievement? This is demonstrated in the story of the donkey: does he walk because he is being hit with a stick or getting to eat the carrot? Think about skills you feel you have not developed as a result of childhood experiences, for example you can't sing, draw or dance.
- Use the skills of the Special Needs Co-ordinator (SENCO) or the local advisory services to talk about how children learn and what is an acceptable rate of progress. If you have concerns about a child's development, collect observations and evidence to support your concerns. Any issues must be discussed with parents/carers before any formal external contact is made.

5. Emotions

Young babies enjoy the company of others, and also need to feel safe and loved when they are not the centre of adult attention.

(*Birth to Three Matters*)

Babies

Babies are born into a social world, a hierarchy of the family and later day care. Generally, they enjoy the stimulation and the company of others. However, it can be a source of worry and tension for some. Being able to get on with others is a complex experience, and babies need to feel safe, knowing they have high levels of love, before feeling secure with new people. Social contact begins with parallel play – playing alongside and watching but not engaging with each other. Play moves on to interactive and co-operative play, making special friends. Babies display pleasure when they see, hear or touch other babies and adults by smiling, making gestures, babbling and eye contact.

Practical activities

- Cradle a baby and move around the setting introducing her to other babies or watching toddlers play.
- Lie two babies side by side and observe how they make contact. Give each one a toy and see how they respond. Do they communicate with sounds, gestures and smiles? Do they reach out towards each other?

- Observe how two babies share the contents of a basket. Fill the basket with interesting items, such as wooden spoons, rattles, soft toys.

- Babies can display care and attention to other babies even at times when they are not the centre of attention. Praise this when it happens and capture with photographs. Add a caption to explain and summarise the scenario.

Toddlers

Toddlers who attend day care or childminders will inevitably be in the company of others, sometimes for the first time. They watch their peers, copy them, and learn from them. Having others around means they will have to compete for attention but it also gives them an audience. 'The terrible twos' refers to the tantrums that erupt during this time; it is a stormy period of getting to grips with strong emotions. The young children develop a range of strategies for getting attention, which include stamping and shouting, floods of tears, becoming manipulative, disruptive or naughty. They will engage all their personal tools: gestures, body language, sounds and words. As they begin to fit into the group, they discover that others have needs and feelings too and that their behaviour and actions have consequences.

Practical activities

- Make snack time a sociable occasion through active participation, passing bowls and plates, saying 'please' and 'thank you'. Often children will try new foods when in a social situations where they observe others' reactions.

- Provide a microphone (or a pretend one) to encourage children to take turns to speak in a small group. Use gestures such as zipping lips to signal to the rest of the group the need to listen and not speak.

- Give each toddler a flag with his name on it and his photograph. If they want adult help let them wave the flag without shouting for attention. Alternatively place some coloured lights or torches in different areas of the room. If they need help, flash the on/off button to get attention.

- Introduce circular mats to define a play area. This makes toddlers feel physically comfortable and settled.

- Ring games, where children hold hands, help them feel secure and cared for; however, limit the size of the ring as too many in the group can be a struggle for some children. Introduce toys and props to vary traditional games and maintain interest.

- Explain that there are times, in emergencies, when things have to be dealt with very quickly and immediately. The adult may have to 'drop everything' to attend to it and others have to wait. Set up role-play situations such as a fire station, police station or hospital.

- When a child is away sick send a 'Get Well' card, a tape-recorded message or e-mail if you have that facility. On his return, make sure he receives a warm welcome back.

Outcomes for the child

- Feeling of self-assurance.
- Self-esteem raised.
- Being able to trust and rely on own abilities.

Focus points

It is important that even young babies understand they cannot be the centre of attention at all times, and they are given time to develop independence. Plan times where pairs or trios can play together. The key carer can use this time to observe attention levels and the development of socialisation. Sometimes, when one baby cries they all join in. Mental and emotional needs are not always obvious but it is important to notice any sudden behavioural changes. If you explain to a child who is demanding attention at an inappropriate time that you are busy but will see him later, make sure you do.

Staff discussion

- Do you have an agreed policy on how to deal with temper tantrums and apply the strategies consistently?
- Plan the room layout so that there are safe areas for socialising and where staff can observe in an unobtrusive way.

6. Planning and resourcing

Note how you prepare for and resource playful activities for young children [babies] to engage in independently.

(Birth to Three Matters)

 Babies

It takes a skilful and reflective practitioner to resource and present a consistently high quality baby room. Helping babies to become independent and self-confident requires the provision of interesting choices that are built into the programme. Getting the balance between too much or not enough is often a problem. Resources need to be presented in ways that will capture babies' attention and interest. They need variety, yet stability, and opportunities where they can explore new experiences safely and in their own time.

Practical activities

- Secure a pine curtain pole safely, about one foot from the floor. This will serve as a pull up bar and help babies to become more independent. Thread rattles, keys, bracelets and jingle jangles onto the pole. This gives the baby the opportunity to play with the object of her choice, whenever she wishes.

- Place plastic water bottles (discovery bottles) containing bright items such as marbles, sparkly beads, sequins, pom-poms, or dried beans, onto place mats at a slight distance from the baby and encourage her to move towards them and choose one for herself.

> **Caution:** Ensure the tops are glued securely onto bottles so that the contents cannot fall out and be swallowed.

- Look for interesting and inviting ways to present the activities. Use food trays, textured or bamboo place mats, patterned felt squares (available from HobbyCraft).

- Explore how you can use the low-level wall area to fix textures that the babies can touch. Also look for easy, accessible open storage units with lightweight, transparent containers so the babies can find things for themselves.

Toddlers

There are often dilemmas for adults when they consider offering toddlers and young children independence. They know children should have it but it means autonomy, choice and self-selection. Some adults find this way of working difficult as they prefer to direct children and be in control. Giving children too much choice can overwhelm them and be non-productive. With increased mobility toddlers become more independent and less reliant on others; the whole environment can become accessible. Toddlers are naturally curious and enjoy exploring and investigating. Facilitating this instinct helps them to become independent and to follow their interests. Inevitably, there will be messy times and at some point, staff will need to intervene. Judging the appropriate moment takes skill and understanding. If too many toys are strewn on the floor, this can be a safety issue with children tripping and falling over. Preparing the environment for independence takes careful consideration about the opportunities offered. For example, resources need to be clearly labelled with symbols, pictures or photographs of the contents, storage needs to be accessible and large clear areas created for floor play.

Practical activities

- Provide play boundaries such as large circular builders' trays, available from DIY stores, to contain resources. It will restrict the spread of construction blocks across the room. Alternatively, they can provide sand play for a small group.

- Store choosing items in vegetable racks. As these racks are open they are easy for a young child to see and access the contents and to tidy back to. These racks are also good for storing water tray toys as they allow them to drip dry.

Laminate labels so that the children can identify where to find/replace contents.

- Look for large plastic sweet jars, storage jars without lids, and food dip trays so that children can choose freely.
- Use large plastic place mats (A3 size, rather than the smaller wooden A4 ones) as this gives each child sufficient space to work.

Outcomes for the child

- Children feel safe, welcome and secure in their environment.
- Daily stimulation to encourage curiosity and exploration.
- The development of self-assurance and independence.

Focus points

Preparation and organisation takes planning and time. It needs to be carefully thought through. An attractive and stimulating environment gives the message that the setting respects and values the children and the staff. In order to present a welcoming environment, with carefully chosen resources and well-presented activities, staff time may need to be reorganised.

Staff discussion

- Regularly review resources, check them, clean, replace and update. Remove clutter and discard broken toys or items with missing parts. This audit helps to remind staff what is available and where it is located, making resourcing more effective.
- Explore Pound shops, kitchen suppliers and hobby shops for a new slant on resources. Stand back and look at the environment with a child's eye.
- Are the designs and resourcing different for babies and toddlers? Do they reflect their differing needs and interests as well as their skills and abilities? As a staff take a new look at where things are and why. Is the environment adult led or child led? Is it child friendly?

References

Dennison, P. (1994) *'Brain Gym': Teacher's Edition (Revised).* London: Body Balance Books.

DfES (Department for Education and Skills) (2002) *Birth to Three Matters: A Framework to Support Children in their Earliest Years.* London: DfES.

DfES (Department for Education and Skills) (2003) *Every Child Matters.* London: DfES.

DfES (Department for Education and Skills)/DWP (Department for Work and Pension) (2003) *National Standards for Under 8s Day Care and Childminding (Full Day Care).* London: DfES.

Conclusion

This book helps to meet the current need to develop guidelines and training materials for early year's practitioners. Its aim is to raise awareness and understanding of practitioners and parents alike in the importance of developing children's well-being and helping them to become emotionally strong. Practitioners have a very important role in the development of a child's well-being that should never be underestimated.

The chapters provide practical activities and ideas for reflection or to promote discussion. Planning and resourcing activities that have well-being in mind ensures that quality time is made for every child and that the practitioner has assimilated the benefits for the child. The behaviour and attitudes of others has a real impact on the self-esteem of both babies and young children. They need to relate well with one another whilst valuing themselves and respecting others. Sound foundations in well-being give children an excellent start in life by helping them to become strong with emotional stability and resilience and have realistic expectations for the future.